W9-AYV-570

As we finished high school
and got ready to leave home,
Mom would give each of us an apron
with the strings cut.

—Anonymous

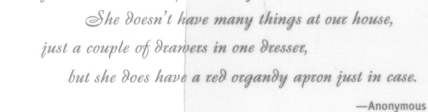

My mom comes and spends every winter with us.
She doesn't have many things at our house,
just a couple of drawers in one dresser,
but she does have a red organdy apron just in case.

—Anonymous

In America, in a tenement flat,
my grandmother wore one apron and over it another,
to keep the first one clean for when company came.

—E. Shakir, Lebanese author and professor

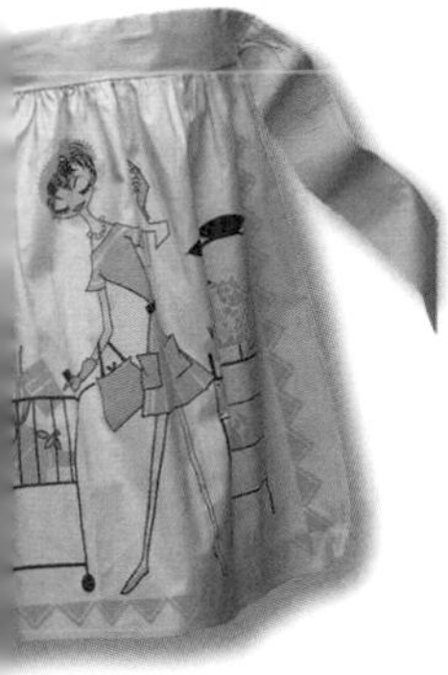

391.44 Che
Aprons : icons of the
American home
Cheney, Joyce.

Aprons

© 2000 by Joyce Cheney
All rights reserved under the Pan-American
and International Copyright Conventions
Printed in China

This book may not be reproduced in whole or in part, in any form or by any means, electronic or mechanical, including photocopying, recording, or by any information storage and retrieval system now known or hereafter invented, without written permission from the publisher.

9 8 7 6 5 4 3 2 1
Digit on the right indicates the number of this printing

Library of Congress Cataloging-in-Publication Number 99-75093

ISBN 0-7624-0694-1

Cover and interior design by Bryn Ashburn
Edited by Laura A. Giuliani and Mary McGuire Ruggiero
Typography: Bauer Bodoni, Bodoni, Boulevard, Gill Sans, Goudy, Officina, and Trixie.

This book may be ordered by mail from the publisher.
Please include $2.50 for postage and handling.
But try your bookstore first!

Running Press Book Publishers
125 South Twenty-second Street
Philadelphia, Pennsylvania 19103-4399

Visit us on the web!
www.runningpress.com

Aprons

Icons of the American Home

by Joyce Cheney

WASHINGTON COUNTY PUBLIC LIBRARY
205 Oak Hill Street
Abingdon, VA 24210

RUNNING PRESS
PHILADELPHIA • LONDON

To Nancy Ann, Carol,
Minger, and Patty;
my mom, big sister,
and grandmothers.

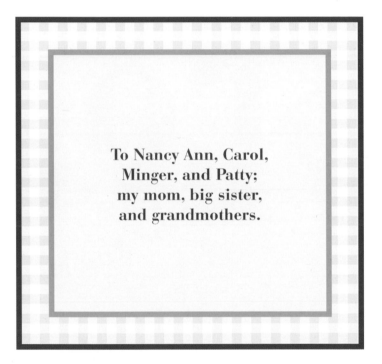

Contents

Preface 6

Introduction 10

Aprons Throughout History..............11
Aprons in America..............15
About Aprons Today...21

Anatomy of an Apron 22

Form..............23
Fabric..............23
Shape..............39
Decoration..............45
Homemade Styles..........68
Store-bought Styles..............76
Function..............81
Work Aprons..............81
Ceremonial and Symbolic Aprons 87
Novelty Aprons 100
Children's Aprons 108
Objets d'art 111

Unfolding an Apron's History 120

Glossary 142

Related Reading 142

Acknowledgments 143

About the Author 144

Photo Credits 144

PREFACE

I love aprons because they remind me of my mother. Aprons signaled the entrance into my mother's world, a world which I was going to inhabit, a world of women. When I was little, I'd climb on a stool to help my mother with the dishes; she would tie one of her aprons around me, up under my armpits so I wouldn't trip on its strings. Later, when I had grown, we'd put on aprons to cook together. Aprons linked us not only in the kitchen, but also through another activity which we both enjoyed: sewing. In the junior high school home economics class that girls were required to take, my first sewing project was an apron—but I already knew how to sew because my mother had taught me. A stickler for detail, she expected that in "addition to pinning and sewing, we'd baste, line, and interface as well.

In the summer of 1989, an outdoor apron display reminded me of apron memories, and offered a way to combine my longtime interests in women's culture and textiles. At a women's festival in the Missouri Ozarks, a Kansas woman hung her apron collection on a clothesline that wandered through the oak woods. Every one of those aprons had been touched, by women, in the making and the wearing. Some conjured images of women stitching the seams and rickrack at old black sewing machines; others, of women sitting on sofas at night, bending into the lamplight to work the embroidery. Those aprons had been stretched across the bellies of working women who wiped their strong and capable hands across the fabric, bringing a swatch of beauty to the tasks of the day.

The next spring, I started collecting aprons, and soon I was on a first-name basis with volunteers at every Goodwill and second-hand store around. I also began to explore other aspects of the textiles. From Laura Brown, a textile conservator, I learned how to look at an apron and decipher its story, to ask questions that might unearth the apron's biography: How is the apron stitched and decorated? Where and why does it show use and wear? How old are the materials? Joile Mackney, owner of St. Louis' The Vintage Haberdashery, further expanded such routes of interpretation with her crash course in fashion history. Julia Samerdyke of the Missouri Historical Society showed me the Society's collection of aprons gathered from Western Expansion days. Since St. Louis was The Gateway to the West—the beginning of the Santa Fe Trail and the Lewis and Clark Trail—many pioneers packed their wagons there before heading west, often jettisoning non-essentials like extra aprons as they condensed their loads.

Beth Alberty, curator of New York's 1989 Metropolitan Museum of Art exhibit "Apropos Aprons," showed her views on aprons as sexual status symbols. Then she sent me to Rosalie Utterbach, Vilma Matchette, and Louise Coffee-Webb, fashion curators responsible for Woodbury University's (Burbank, California) 1990 apron show, "Ties that Bind." These women believe in conserving the ordinary, and organized the apron show as part of a series of exhibits of the daily wear of the average citizen including cotton housedresses, rain gear, men's hand-painted Forties ties, and buttons. David Colker of the *Los Angeles Times* reviewed "Ties That Bind," and learned that the women were onto something. Although Colker had initially resented the assignment—*an apron show?*—he actually loved the exhibit, and had to be ushered from the gallery when it closed, not wanting to end his three-hour experience of aprons. Discovering several contemporary artists who work with aprons further inspired me. Clearly these artists have recognized the strength of aprons as symbols.

In the summer of 1994, I decided to express my own understanding of aprons by arranging a display at Ghost Ranch in Abiquiu, New Mexico. One morning at sunrise, early risers found twenty-six freshly ironed aprons flapping on a clothesline strung between two trees. To my surprise, people wanted not only to look at the aprons but to touch them, try them on, and linger nearby the clothesline. Two things encouraged me to continue collecting and sharing aprons: the first was watching a mother and her

Dear Joyce,

Seeing your clothesline with aprons flapping in the breeze at Ghost Ranch was an eye opener and a healer for me. I'm enclosing an apron for your collection, made by my mom about 30 years ago. I'd like to tell you about her, my reaction to her aprons, and what I learned today.

Her name was Gertie and she died at 77, twelve years ago. When she was 50 she took a part-time job as a grade school cook, but cooking was an important part of her life long before that. She was a good cook and meals had a rhythm: always at seven, noon, and five. Just like washday was always Monday, and clean clothes were hanging on the line by 8 a.m. I've often evaluated myself by those standards.

She always wore a full apron because a half-apron "doesn't keep you clean when you cook." I hated those aprons. When I was younger, I thought they made my mother look dumpy because she was somewhat overweight and had a large bosom (as she would say). When I was in my twenties in the feminist-strengthening Seventies, I hated her aprons because they meant for me the absence of dreams outside the home. They were definitely not "in," nor was she.

She was very particular with her aprons, and wore a fresh one every day. They were sharply starched and pressed (as were sheets and dish towels as well as all our clothes). She sewed new aprons whenever the current ones showed signs of wear.

It seemed there was a strong and regular rhythm to her life. I resisted and rebelled at it all—that's why it was so odd that I chose to save six of her aprons when she died and we were going through her things. I never really thought about why I took those aprons, only that I couldn't bear to have them thrown away or sold for $.50 at a garage sale.

So for all these years since her death they've been in our basement. Seeing people touch and appreciate your aprons, and hearing you talk excitedly about women's aprons clicked a switch in me, and transformed part of her life for me, and transformed part of my life through her as well. I feel a softening in a new place where hardness had been. I wish you could have met her. She was quite a strong, determined, spiritual lady, and so is her daughter.

Thank you, Gertie.

From Karen Holseth-Broekema,
Neshkoro, Wisconsin, July 1994

two children view the aprons, the children asking, "what are they?"; the other was a touching letter received after the exhibit (see opposite page).

Inspired by such a response, I continued and increased my collecting so that in 1996 I was able to organize an exhibition of more than 250 aprons in St. Louis. The exhibit exceeded everyone's—our own and the viewers'—expectations: "Why didn't I think of this?" "Look at this one; I used to have one just like it." "We've got to come back and bring Aunt Lucy." Only one visitor panned the exhibit, writing "Aprons are uniforms of oppression!" in the guest book, and I suppose from one narrow perspective they are. But they are also manifestations of resourcefulness, artifacts of important work, and examples of creativity, which are simply enjoyable to look at. These are the attributes which I have discovered in aprons, which I find empowering and poignant, and which I want to share with others.

I submitted a touring exhibit proposal to ExhibitsUSA, and included a few aprons along with the application. The judges passed the aprons around the boardroom, telling their own apron stories, and quickly announced their vote to launch a national tour. Once the tour began, this book took shape, pieced together from the apron stories gathered at exhibits, church suppers, and women's clubs, among other locales. I hope *Aprons* piques your interest in this unique textile icon and motivates you to gather your own family's aprons and apron stories.

INTRODUCTION

The power of aprons lies in how they make us feel and what they help us to remember. For many, aprons are nostalgic. They represent being loved and loving others, security, stability, simpler times, and very different times—components of an American Dream that includes apple pie and white picket fences. Not all of us lived like the Cleavers, of course, but the significance of aprons is nevertheless based on something stronger than historical fact—a sort of mythology, a collective source of memories and feelings, a social fabric, if you will.

Aprons provide direct ties to our personal and shared histories. The housewife and the hired help, the server and the served, the slave and the mistress all wore aprons. The women in each of our families have worn them—if not us, then our mothers or their mothers or theirs, and for that matter, more than a few fathers and grandfathers as well. Aprons surface around the world, throughout the centuries, and across the great demographic divides. The symbolism of aprons reflects such a vast profile; people wear aprons to keep clean, to advertise their status, to catch another's eye, or simply for pleasure. Not every apron tells a rosy story—some tell of hard work, unfairness, or even cruelty. Nevertheless, each apron recalls a time and a place, a story and a face; it is because of these important ties that we must treasure our aprons and recognize the threads which they sew among us and the stories they tell about us.

Aprons Throughout History

Aprons tap into our personal memories and remind us of mothers, grandmothers, and our own pasts. They serve as symbols of home, motherhood, and housewifery, from images of a colonial woman fanning the cooking fire with her long apron, to a Civil War nurse wearing her white apron on the battlefield, to a country mother during the depression gathering potatoes in her tattered apron, to a Fifties housewife wearing a ruffled and rickracked apron to serve dinner. Women have moved in and out of having servants or doing housework themselves, and in and out of the labor market. Those changes have been reflected in their aprons. Yet the history of aprons extends beyond women, beyond the borders of this country, and beyond this modern era.

Aprons can be seen in some of the earliest times that visual history has shown us. Cretan fertility goddesses wore sacred aprons; ceremonial aprons were worn by Assyrian priests, and Egyptian rulers wore jewel-encrusted aprons, the shape, placement and folds of which declared specific rank.

The apron tradition in the United States grew from customs in Western Europe, where people have been wearing aprons since the thirteenth century. At that time and through the Middle Ages (circa A.D. 500 to 1500), meals were often communal affairs, with diners literally grabbing food and eating by hand. Women typically placed an extra swath of cloth in their laps to protect their skirts while eating, creating a sort of banquet apron.

{Adam and Eve} sewed fig leaves together, and made themselves aprons.

–*Bible*: Genesis 3:7

By the Middle Ages, many tradespeople wore aprons as protective workwear. Blacksmiths wore leather aprons. The most massive styles were two-paneled coverings that protected the smithy front and back, neck to toe. More commonly, smithies covered the front of their torso and legs by wearing a whole animal hide, one shank serving as a bib, buttoned to the garment beneath through a hole slashed into the leather.

Tanners had to protect their own flesh from the strong, acidic brews they used on animal hides, so they wore leg guards below their short pants, plus two layers of aprons. Against their clothing they wore a thick sheepskin half apron tied at the waist, and over that a leather apron, which extended from neck to knees.

Garbage picking, a livelihood practiced mainly by poor women during the Middle Ages, required protective gear. A picker would climb atop piles of refuse, plunging her sieve into the mix and filling the scoop as she pushed it away from her body. Then, with as much force as she could muster, she'd pull the sieve back towards her and abruptly whack it against her body, forcing smaller debris out and revealing whatever she'd culled. Obviously, her heavy full-length leather apron was a safety necessity.

Workers such as fishermen who needed protection from moisture, wore aprons of oilskin, a coarse cotton soaked with oil. Some fishermen preferred aprons of heavy wool, which was thick and absorbed moisture. Wool also made a good surface for wiping oily fish scales off one's hands.

While workers who needed to shield their bodies were among the first to wear aprons, eventually higher standards of cleanliness and easier access to cloth converged, and both tradespeople and artisans began wearing aprons to protect their clothing.

"The fishmonger pulls off his hat and his men cleanse their fingers on their woolen aprons."

—FROM *OUR MUTUAL FRIEND*
BY CHARLES DICKENS
ENGLISH NOVELIST (1812–1870)

The most basic fabric aprons were simply pieces of cloth held on by whatever means were available— tucked into the waist of a wearer's pants or skirt, cinched with a belt or piece of twine, or simply tied on using the corners of the fabric. Eventually, fabric apron design became more complex, and waistbands and ties or strings became the norm. The first fabric apron bibs were short, extending only a few inches upward from the waist and were fastened in place with pins or buttons. Bibs with neck straps were the next design improvement.

The archaic term "apron men" means tradesmen in general, and comes from a time when aprons were so common that several trades boasted distinguishing styles. Though there were certainly variations across geography and time, in general, gardeners, spinners, weavers, and garbage men wore blue aprons; butlers wore green; butchers wore blue stripes; cobblers wore "black flag" aprons for protection from the black wax they used, and English barbers were known as "checkered apron men." Stone masons wore white aprons to blend with the white dust of their trade, and even today, leaders of the Mason's fraternal society wear aprons during their ceremonies.

Women wore aprons as they tilled soil, milked cows, scaled fish, baked bread, brewed ale, sold or delivered their wares and completed all the other chores that were part of their daily, domestic duties. Their functional aprons were plain, usually of linen or cotton and occasionally of leather, and ranged from short half-apron to full-length bibbed styles. Their purpose was to protect the wearer's clothing, and sometimes a woman wore two half

Speak, what trade art thou?
Why, sir, a carpenter.
Where is thy leather apron
and thy rule?

—from *Julius Caesar*
by William Shakespeare (1564–1616)
English poet and dramatist

aprons, tying one in the front and one in the back to protect more of her dress beneath. In addition to ties around the waist and neck, some full aprons had as many as three additional ties to hold the skirt in place and thus provide better protection. Sometimes a woman even tied a piece of old sacking over her apron, to protect the apron itself from wear.

When women began working for wages—or for room and board—they continued to wear aprons on the job. Most working women's aprons were white, but there were some exceptions. Some cooks wore blue or white, and some chambermaids wore blue and white checks for most chores but white when changing bed linens. Nurses wore dark colored aprons to minimize washings but switched to white as hygienic standards tightened, and doctors wore white aprons before switching to the white lab coats worn today. Women who worked in the textile mills and other early factories wore aprons, as well as scarves covering their hair and kerchiefs over their mouths and noses to protect themselves from inhaling dust so thick that it was said to limit workers' views to only a few feet.

By the beginning of the sixteenth century, decorative aprons were becoming fashion accessories for European women with lifestyles permitting such luxury and display. As these privileged women's lives became more comfortable and leisurely, their aprons grew more elaborate, with embroidery, lace, ribbons and other luxuries removing any doubt as to the wearer's financial and social status. Even noblewomen wore aprons when styles dictated. Children of the rich and famous wore aprons too; boys until about seven, girls until the age at which they began dressing in adult garb. These children's aprons were usually bibbed pinafores, and served both as protective and decorative garments.

Aprons remained popular accessories throughout the seventeenth, eighteenth, and nineteenth centuries. Because the design of these aprons was dictated by fashion rather than practical necessity, styles changed as often as that of other garments of the well-to-do. They became shorter or longer, fuller or narrower, subtle, or attention-getting. And like other garments at the mercy of fashion whims, the decorative aprons' popularity waxed and waned, with heavily decorated aprons being most common during the Victorian era (mid-1800s to 1900).

The highly decorated aprons that we may think of as part of the "traditional folk costume" are a relatively short-lived aspect of European dress. Until the nineteenth century, most "folk" (by definition the common people living traditional lifestyles) had neither the time nor the resources for elaborate clothing. Decorative regional attire existed, but played a minor role in commoners' dress.

As life became easier for poor people, though, their special locally-unique clothes became more distinctive and elaborate. Aprons and other elements such as hairstyle, head covering, skirt or pants length, or fabric broadcast the specific demographics of the wearer, including locale of origin, religion, age, marital status, or other descriptors. Such regional attire flourished well into the twentieth century in some isolated parts of Europe, until urbanization and mass production of inexpensive clothing resulted in an homogenization of dress.

In Europe today, "traditional folk costumes" including aprons, are most often worn for festivals and ceremonies, and are more likely to be sewn for tourists than to be crafted as a local family's heirloom.

Aprons in America

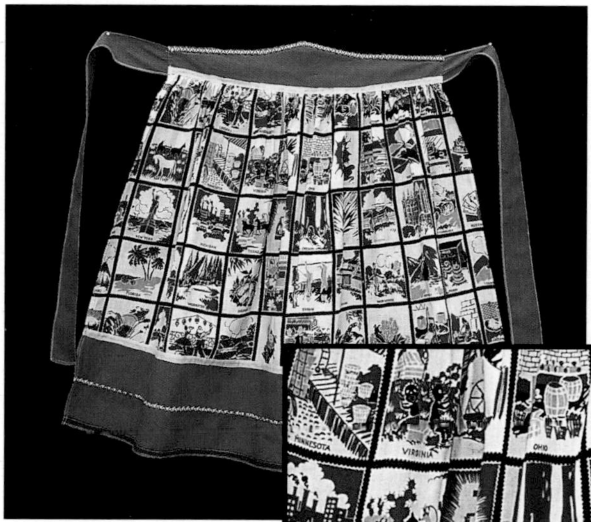

In the United States, aprons seem to possess slightly different connotations, as they have come to symbolize the uniform of domesticity, representing the security and sanctity of home and family. How has such meaning evolved? By the time Europeans settled in North America, aprons were firmly established in women's wardrobes. Though the long white aprons of the colonial women were not practical in color, they were nonetheless very useful. In addition to using their aprons to keep other garments clean, colonial women and their daughters, through the next two centuries, often used their aprons as carriers, gathering the bottom seams in hand to form a pouch for toting vegetables, eggs, laundry, and so forth.

African slaves brought to America also wore aprons. While some slaves sewed their folk tales and family lore onto quilts, others embroidered and patched their stories onto aprons.

In the early 1800s, households produced much of what they needed themselves. In homes where household members could afford hired help, servants performed the necessary labor. In fact, in New York City, one in five households had servants. Amongst the rural dwellers, though, no one escaped hard work, and every woman's apron served as pot holder, fire fan, towel, carrier, and more.

In 1841, Catherine Beecher, sister of Harriet Beecher Stowe who wrote *Uncle Tom's Cabin*, published her *Treatise on Domestic Economy*, a wildly popular text "for the use of young ladies at home and at school" in which the author attempted to redefine and elevate the value of women's work at home. Beecher promoted housework as an "honorable and serious profession, one which requires training and specialized knowledge, one which embraces high responsibilities." She wanted to acknowledge the housewife as the "one in charge of sacred ministries of the family state." When Beecher's ideal housewife wore an apron, then, it signified neither humble work nor frivolous decoration. It was part of the woman's professional uniform, a proud symbol of her status as housewife.

In the second half of the nineteenth century, industrialization began to change how work was done. As technical processes became more complex, specialization developed and work once performed in the home gradually became the bailiwick of outside workers. These changes in work added variety to apron wardrobes. In addition to practical and decorative at-home aprons, more women began to wear aprons for their work in garment factories, hospitals, inns, restaurants, shops and elsewhere. Most people had very few clothes and laundering was grueling work, so aprons were important for the protection of other garments.

In the first decade of the twentieth century, almost every city dweller had cold running water, if only from a faucet in the courtyard. Some cities absorbed thousands of immigrants, many of whom lived in crowded and squalid conditions. Things were, however, easing up for women of means. Those who could afford it bought more goods and services from butchers, bakers, doctors, retailers and others; electricity was just coming in to the fanciest homes; and birth rates were down.

More women became educated and entered the professions. Although women of means were freed from some labors, they had fewer servants than their mothers, and thus more chores to complete themselves. With whatever time they did have, in addition to sewing and embroidering their long, white, delicate decorative aprons, women of means launched a movement called "social housekeeping," in which women took their moral influence and caretaking sensibilities out of the home to address urban social issues and to clean up politics. Many were busy supporting temperance, the suffragist movement, and the provision of housing, education and healthcare for the poor.

During World War I (1914–1918), women saw job options increase as the economy expanded to support the war and as male soldiers went to battle. Women's apron styles began to reflect this change, and women wore a variety of aprons appropriate to their stations, tasks and expanded opportunities. Some wore a new apron style, the Hooverette, which had come out during the war when Herbert Hoover was Food Administrator. It was a wraparound full apron that "covered all of you."

The Twenties was a decade of optimism for the financially well-off, and affluent women seized the chance to expand their options. Young single women dressed as flappers, began to smoke in public, and go on unsupervised dates. Well-heeled women of all ages wore fragile decorative half aprons made of silk, linen or cotton, or full aprons made of sturdy cotton. These full aprons covered the wearer's whole torso front and back and hung loosely, without waist definition, to match the unshaped dresses they covered. Since the Twenties were a time when refined ladies were still expected to possess and display their needlework skills, decorative aprons often had elaborate embroidery or other hand-sewn needlework. Apron embroidery designs became widely available in kits. Seamstresses could buy just the embroidery pattern to apply to an existing apron, or they could buy fabric with lines for cutting, assembling and embroidering an apron already printed on the cloth. In addition, during the Twenties, ready-to-wear clothing became more accessible and acceptable. Central heat, electricity, and labor-saving devices like vacuum cleaners, sewing machines, and washing machines became available to the wealthy. All these changes could have made homemaking less time consuming, but as domestic expectations increased, housewives spent at least as many hours on chores as their mothers had, wearing full aprons of gingham, calico, or other light cottons as they worked.

By the mid-Twenties, farmers nationwide were suffering. Prices were falling for agricultural goods and farmers' debts were climbing. Many historians say that the rural depression began in the mid-Twenties. Then in 1929, the stock market crashed, and the rest of America entered the Great Depression.

For a few wealthy families, this period meant making economic decisions carefully and perhaps doing more charity work. For everyone else, it brought great upheaval and suffering. Two-thirds of the population had incomes below the poverty level. Marriage and birth rates declined. Divorce rates dropped as families stayed together for financial survival, but desertions increased, too.

Labor unions gained a national stronghold in the Thirties and women's membership in unions tripled, although women worked at separate jobs for lower wages. At home, housewives still spent the same time on housework as their mothers and their grandmothers had. Again, the image of womanhood changed to fit the times. The Twenties woman *fulfilled* herself individually or through family; the Thirties woman *sacrificed* for family.

For all women except the most affluent, Thirties aprons were used for hard work. Women's dresses were cut close to con-

GRANT WOOD'S FAMOUS 1930 PAINTING, AMERICAN GOTHIC, SHOWS A FARM COUPLE, THE WIFE WEARING AN APRON. THIS MAY BE THE FIRST RENDERING OF RICKRACK TRIMMING IN FINE ART.

serve fabric, and aprons mirrored those fitted lines. Cloth was available but costly, so women wore aprons until they were threadbare, and some even sewed aprons from feed or flour sacks.

World War II (1941–1945) brought an abrupt end to the Depression and ushered in a booming economy with full employment. Suddenly and miraculously, women were able to do all types of mentally and physically demanding work previously deemed beyond their capabilities, and Rosie the Riveter came to represent those able employees. Rosie liked the challenge and variety of her work, and she liked the respect and the money she earned. At home, Rosie wore aprons made of cotton but she had only one or two, as rationing made cloth scarce at any price. Colors tended toward the dark and intense, and while tiny calico prints were popular, large flower prints were coming into fashion as well. At her outside job, Rosie wore whatever protection the task required, anything from an apron to a jumpsuit, heavy gloves, and welding mask.

The late Forties and the whole decade of the Fifties, the baby boom years, were the heyday of aprons. During a century in which divorce rates had generally risen and birth rates had fallen, the baby boom years were the opposite. Mothers married young and had three to four children—more than their mothers and grandmothers had, and more than their children and grandchildren would have.

Why were families having so many babies? Other economically similar periods had not resulted in the same phenomenon. One theory suggests that the baby boom was in response to multiple social and psychological pressures placed upon women. Mass media, the healthcare industry, government, and educational institutions all touted the benefits of a large family. These institutions encouraged, and in many cases, forced women to give up their wartime jobs and settle for "women's work" both in and out of the home. "Home Sweet Home" was something a middle-class mother could achieve and control, so she applied herself and excelled. Being a homemaker was considered a calling, the most honorable profession for a woman, and an apron became a uniform to be worn with pride.

In the baby boom years many people felt optimistic; they had hope. They believed that life was getting better for everybody and that life would be even better for the children than it had been for the grown-ups. Televisions hit the marketplace in 1950, and this optimism was

When I was in the TV series *Father Knows Best*, I wore a lot of aprons. When the series was over, the aprons went back to Columbia Studio's wardrobe department. Several years later I saw that lovely actress, Ruby Dee, in a film made by Columbia. She was wearing all my aprons. It gave me the oddest feeling!

—Jane Wyatt
American Actress

reflected in the popular television shows of the decade. Ozzie and Harriet Nelson of *Ozzie and Harriet* and Ward and June Cleaver of *Leave it to Beaver* showed America how families should and perhaps could be.

It was a stable time for families for several reasons. Some of that stability was because government support was flowing; 40 percent of men were eligible for the G.I. bill and studied their way to a more comfortable rung on the economic ladder, and employment was high. People wanted things "back to normal." Companies, eager to earn a share of the country's prosperity, launched ad campaigns selling a specific idea of family—a nuclear family surrounded with new products that would ensure their happiness. They found that consumers were eager to buy after nearly two decades of austerity.

During this optimistic time, all kinds of labor-saving appliances were marketed to the middle class housewife, some of which had been available for years but which had finally hit the mass market—washers, dryers, and dishwashers, not to mention hundreds of cleaning products and convenience foods. A baby boom era housewife, using all the gadgets marketed to her, could single-handedly provide a middle-class standard of health and cleanliness for her family, a task that required a housewife plus a staff of three or four to accomplish only one century earlier.

At the same time washers and dryers became mainstream, young women learned sewing skills in home economics classes, and cloth became readily available, decorative aprons were in their prime. Thus, the baby boom years reigned as the zenith of apron wear. In addition to the sturdy ones Mother kept in the kitchen drawer or pantry for everyday, she had a special frilly apron for holidays. Some attribute aprons' ubiquitous popularity in the Fifties to the legitimization of homemaking during that decade, with aprons becoming a type of uniform through which housewives could broadcast their overall professional status as well as their specific sewing skill and creativity.

The end of the Fifties and the beginning of the Sixties were years of relative affluence. In fact, by 1969, poverty was at the lowest level ever measured in America. Yet discontent and a pressure for change was in the air. United States' involvement in the Vietnam war was increasing, the civil rights movement was gaining strength, and feminist forces were beginning to crystallize.

Women made a link between civil rights and women's rights, and they began asking questions, too. Betty Friedan's 1963 book, *The Feminine Mystique*, described "the problem that has no name," the plight of the educated housewife who felt trapped and stifled within the confines of "Home Sweet Home." Many a white, middle-class woman saw herself in Friedan's book. Was she really finding her life's meaning in washing the dishes? Was vacuuming the living room floor or even raising her children enough to challenge her to full capacity? Was housework an expression of social status, familial love, and moral purity, or was it just plain hard work?

With economic changes came the end of the baby boom. Wages began to fall and inflation rose, so people had to live differently in order to maintain their standards of living. They married later, both spouses got jobs, they had fewer children, and many went into debt. White female-headed households skyrocketed and divorces increased. The era—and the dream—of the two-parent family with a stay-at-home mom ended.

During the Sixties, as the era of glorified housework passed, so went the heyday of aprons. Housework continued of course, but without the glamorization of those chores and romanticization of the housewife's role. Women of the Sixties wore aprons similar to those worn in the Fifties. Bold color combinations were popular, both for aprons and kitchens. (Remember refrigerators in harvest gold, avocado green, turquoise, pink, dark brown, and burnt orange?) Overall, though, apron wear became much less common in the Sixties. The apron ceased to be a ubiquitous garment and became instead an occasional accessory, a pop culture symbol of an era passed.

In the Seventies, unemployment and inflation soared, poverty increased sharply, and racial tensions continued. Disillusionment and change continued and a conservative movement grew in response; the Silent Majority wanted things "back to normal" again. But middle-class women didn't, and feminism emerged as a major force in their lives. Changes in women's societal and legislative opportunities and individual lives continued; in fact, change escalated as women postponed marriage and childbearing even longer, stayed in school longer, established new careers and got more divorces. New women's institutions were created, and positive examples of working women such as Mary Tyler Moore showed up on television.

Aprons worn in the Seventies reflected people's various attitudes towards homemaking. Some people felt fine about housewifery and wore decorative aprons that were gaudy, bawdy, and cutsie—just like the clothes of the decade. Other women reached their limits with decorative aprons and what they believed they represented and would don only work aprons. Even practical aprons were worn less as permanent press fabrics became common and laundry was less of a chore. In general, the phasing out of aprons that began in the Sixties continued through the Seventies, and into the next two decades as well.

Women's lives have continued to change. Women marry later and have fewer children, and many are forgoing marriage and simply bearing and raising children on their own. Before World War II, one in six marriages ended in divorce; fifty years later, it's more than one in two. In 1990, more than half of married women worked outside the home. Eighty percent of women work in 5 percent of the jobs, mostly clerical, sales, or service. Blue and white collar job opportunities have expanded somewhat, though. In 1940, 8 percent of medical, business, and law school entrants were female, while in the mid-Eighties, 40 percent of the new students were women, and the trend continues.

About Aprons Today

Today, you won't find aprons in every kitchen. Wash-and-wear clothing or not, however, it makes sense to have something handy to wipe your hands on, to hold items in, or to use to catch spills. Not surprisingly, functional aprons are still worn by workers, including food preparers and servers, retail clerks, street vendors, ticket sellers, daycare workers, morticians, artisans, fishermen, and many others who work with their hands.

Aprons serve two main functions today. First, they remain pop culture symbols, shorthand for motherhood, family, and domesticity as romanticized in the Fifties, though opinions vary as to whether the lifestyle that aprons have come to symbolize is "good" or "bad." Regardless of one's position on this issue, aprons are indisputable icons of women's creativity and resourcefulness. Second, aprons today serve as uniforms—just look at the servers in any fast food chain, discount store, or quick stop. But gone is the variety, the visual delight, and the individual expression of aprons.

As for decorative aprons, they're not exactly a current fashion trend, but anything can happen in the fashion world. Occasionally throughout the Nineties an apron look has surfaced on a New York runway, but none of those looks has caught on. (We'll know that the apron has re-emerged as a hot, must-have accessory when Calvin Klein ads feature some hardbody wearing an apron and nothing else.) Until then, hang a couple of sturdy favorites in the kitchen for everyday use and save a fancy one in a drawer for dress-up, just in case. And the next time you go through those boxes in the basement, look for aprons; or the next time your whole family gathers, ask about aprons, and listen for the stories that those aprons conjure up.

Today's aprons are generally confined to one cut, the gender-generic full-length barbecue apron. But there are some interesting specialty twists such as the photographer's darkroom apron with a cuff at the bottom to catch any toxic liquid that might run down, or the wood shop apron with a thin pencil pocket sewn on the bib and attached only at the top so that when the wearer leans forward, the bottom of the pocket swings free and the pencils don't fall out.

Anatomy of an Apron

At its most basic, an apron is just a covering for the front of one's clothes. Here is a look at how seamstresses have approached this simple design challenge and what the resulting aprons reflect about ourselves and our society.

Form

FABRIC

Some aprons are noteworthy for the materials from which they are made. Aprons have been sewn of cotton, synthetics, linen, silk, plastic, and paper. Specialized aprons have been made of leather, rubber, heat- or chemical-protective synthetics, and even lead (that heavy apron that's still placed on you before your teeth are x-rayed). But most of us recall cotton aprons.

While some seamstresses purchased fabric specifically for making aprons, not everyone had that luxury. Other women recycled used items into aprons, or they pieced sewing scraps together, producing aprons that mirrored the whole family's homemade wardrobe. Is your family one of the many that wore aprons made from flour, sugar or feed sacks in the Thirties and Forties? Many sacks came dyed and printed for conversion into clothing.

For decades, women have made aprons out of towels, or they've sewn hand towels to the front of plain cotton aprons for serious hand wiping. While "barbecue aprons" are the style most commonly for sale today, terry cloth aprons account for most of the half aprons still available.

Aprons are women's voices

that were mute.

—Ellen Rulseh
American journalist
and performer

upper left apron: Apron made from a commercially made dishrag with hand-crocheted borders and pocket added. The bright colors suggest that it's from the Fifties.
upper right: Thirties or Forties apron made from a sugar sack.
lower right: Apron made of red guest hand towel with ribbon waistband and embroidery added from the Fifties or Sixties.
lower left: Fifties colors are featured in this apron made of white utility dishtowel with bias tape trim.

Lbs. Net
Fine
Granulated
Cane Sugar

opposite: This reversible apron, made of printed flour sacks, was worn with a molded plastic waistband briefly popular in the Fifties.
above: This Seventies apron is assembled from men's silk and synthetic neckties from earlier decades.

As we finished high school

and got ready to leave home,

mom would give each of us

an apron

with the strings cut.

—Anonymous

opposite: Handkerchief aprons were popular throughout the Forties, Fifties, and Sixties. Most were half-aprons made completely from three or four cotton hankies. Handkerchiefs were also used as pockets, borders or other decorations on aprons made of other fabrics.

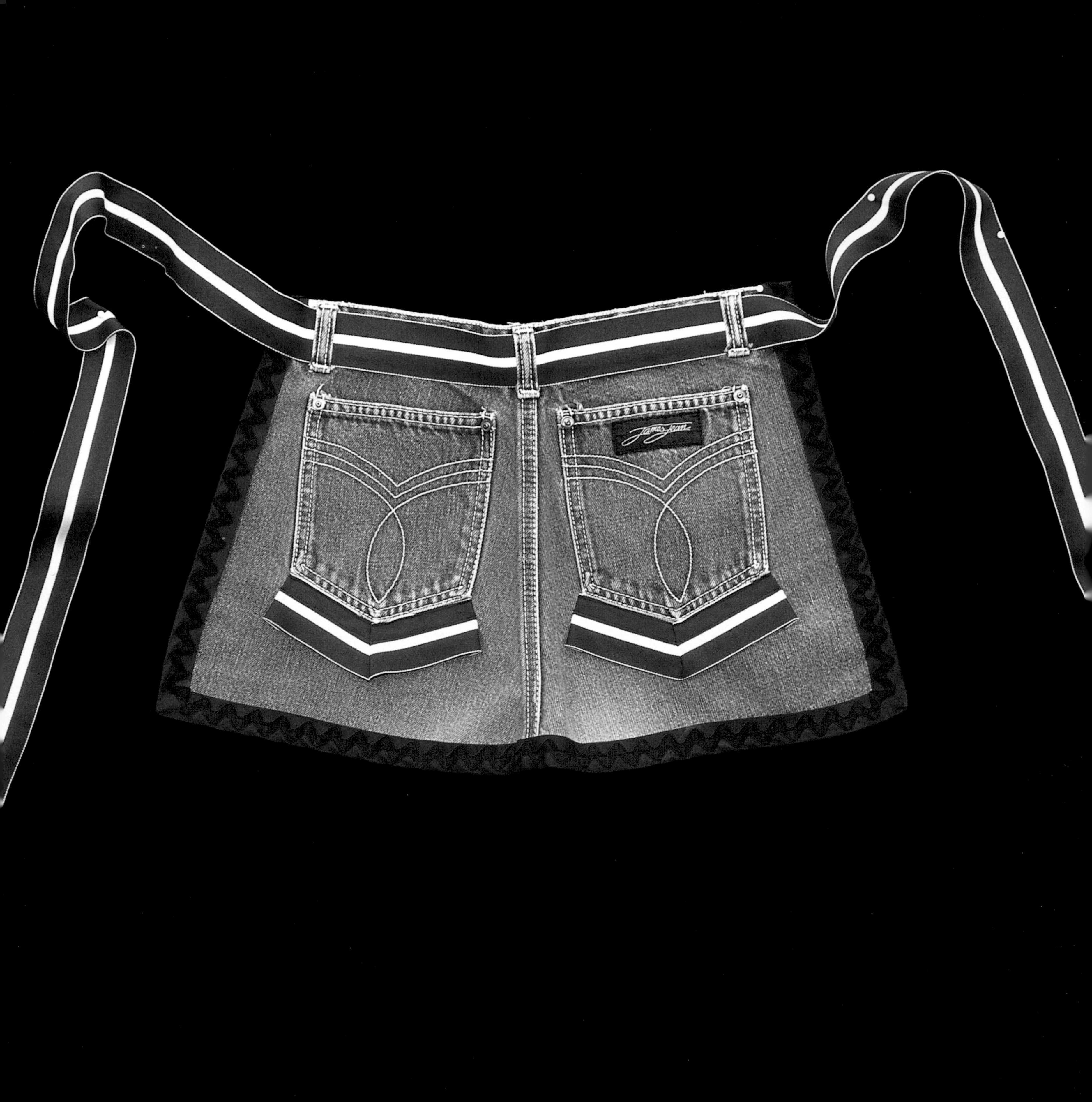

Authentic 1990s' women still wear aprons. I often wonder if the suffragettes collectively would be proud of American women today—proud that we are wearing Levis under our aprons and that some of us are breaking six-figure salaries.

—Gabrielle McGraw
American cyberwriter, contributor to the online magazine, *The Case Against*

opposite: This Seventies apron is made from the seat of an actual pair of denim blue jeans, with rickrack and ribbon ties added.

above: This cotton apron was sewn in the Fifties, judging from the rickrack and the fabric of the patches. Note that the bib has no neck strap and is pinned to the store-bought house dress from the Fifties or Sixties.

above: This cotton apron is made of patches carefully chosen to blend color and tone. Patchwork creations such as this can be hard to date, as seamstresses may have collected scraps over several years—or decades—before assembling them into something new.

I made these aprons,

and they were so beautiful I thought what a shame nobody can see them, so I took them over to the tea room and hung them, up and they sold out in a matter of hours.

—Claudia McGraw
Owner of The Apron Lady tea room and
apron designer for Greta Garbo, Lyndon Johnson's
daughter Luci, and Amy Vanderbilt

opposite: This Fifties apron is made of heavy cotton canvas. The embroidery must have been from a pattern, as the same design was found on other aprons.

What do aprons represent? I ask myself.

Domesticity, docility, a readiness for messy work.

What do aprons conceal?

The body's most interesting areas.

—Jeannette Batz
American Journalist and Author

opposite: The skirt of this Seventies apron consists of a front layer of clear plastic and a back layer of netting, with plastic fruit glued in between. Ribbon is used for waistband, ties, and skirt edging.

LURLINE

SHAPE

How many ways can flat cloth be shaped and arranged to protect and adorn? For a creative seamstress, the possibilities are many. Full aprons are like sculptures as they curve over and around the body; half aprons are more like two-dimensional paintings.

For [domestic workers in the early 1900s]

the apron

was a convenient, all-purpose tool,
used to carry wood and kindling,
to gather eggs and vegetables,
to wipe their brows in the noon-day sun,
or just to hide a special treat
for a willing helper.

—FROM *MA DEAR'S APRONS*
BY PATRICIA C. MCKISSACK
AMERICAN AUTHOR

upper left: This brown child's apron is a flat rectangle gathered by a same-fabric band slipped through a casing at the top. The cotton-polyester blend suggests it was made in the Sixties or later.
upper right: Aprons constructed from triangular pieces of fabric called gores, were common during the Thirties, Forties, and Fifties, and allowed seamstresses to play with cloth mixtures. This apron alternates solid cloth with Hawaiian-themed fabric, popular after World War II.
bottom: This cotton scalloped apron, bound with bias tape and cut for a large woman, has colors and print characteristic of the Forties.

opposite: This sheer cotton apron from the Thirties or Forties has multi-tiered gathers with embroidered flowers and edging.
above: Ballet dancers in full skirts adorn this cotton apron cut very full to cover a Fifties full skirt and to reproduce the dancers' motion.

above: The angular print of this late-Forties cotton apron is well-suited to its shape.

opposite: The shapes and fastening choices of full apron backs are at least as interesting as the design of the fronts. This general style—loose-fitting, cotton full-length, full bibbed apron with no waist—was common in both commercial and homemade versions from the Thirties through the Seventies, and was almost universally worn for serious housework in the Forties and Fifties. Because so many grandmothers wore them, this type of apron has been nicknamed the "Grandma Apron."

DECORATION

Once a seamstress has accomplished the basic task of designing an apron, she uses a variety of decorative materials to creatively express herself.

In the Fifties, the ever-prepared hostess had several aprons to match her outfits or even to match the placemats. Bright colors were in vogue and synthetics were becoming available, so women collected large apron wardrobes ranging from sedate calico full aprons to sheer half aprons festooned with rickrack, sequin, ribbons, pompoms, plastic fruit, and more.

opposite: This Fifties apron must have been made from a pattern, as two exact versions were discovered, one in Missouri and one in California. The burlap apron has a ribbon waist, felt pocket, and grapes made of felt, pompoms, and pipe cleaners.

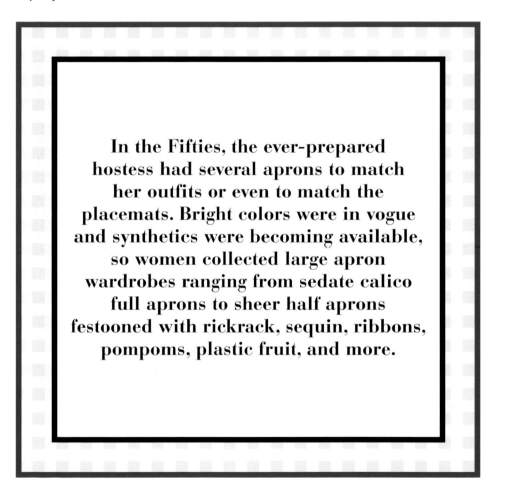

opposite: This Twenties apron made from a kit is embellished with embroidery and hand-painting. Although hand-painting remained popular through the Forties, this dress's shape—cut straight to go over the long, narrow dresses of that decade–is what dates it.

She drew her lace unceasing. . . . She had the strength and sang-froid of a woman in the prime of life. She continued drawing the lace with slow, dignified movements. The big web came up inevitably over her apron; the length of lace fell away at her side.

—from *Sons and Lovers*
by D. H. Lawrence (1885–1930)
English novelist, short-story writer, poet

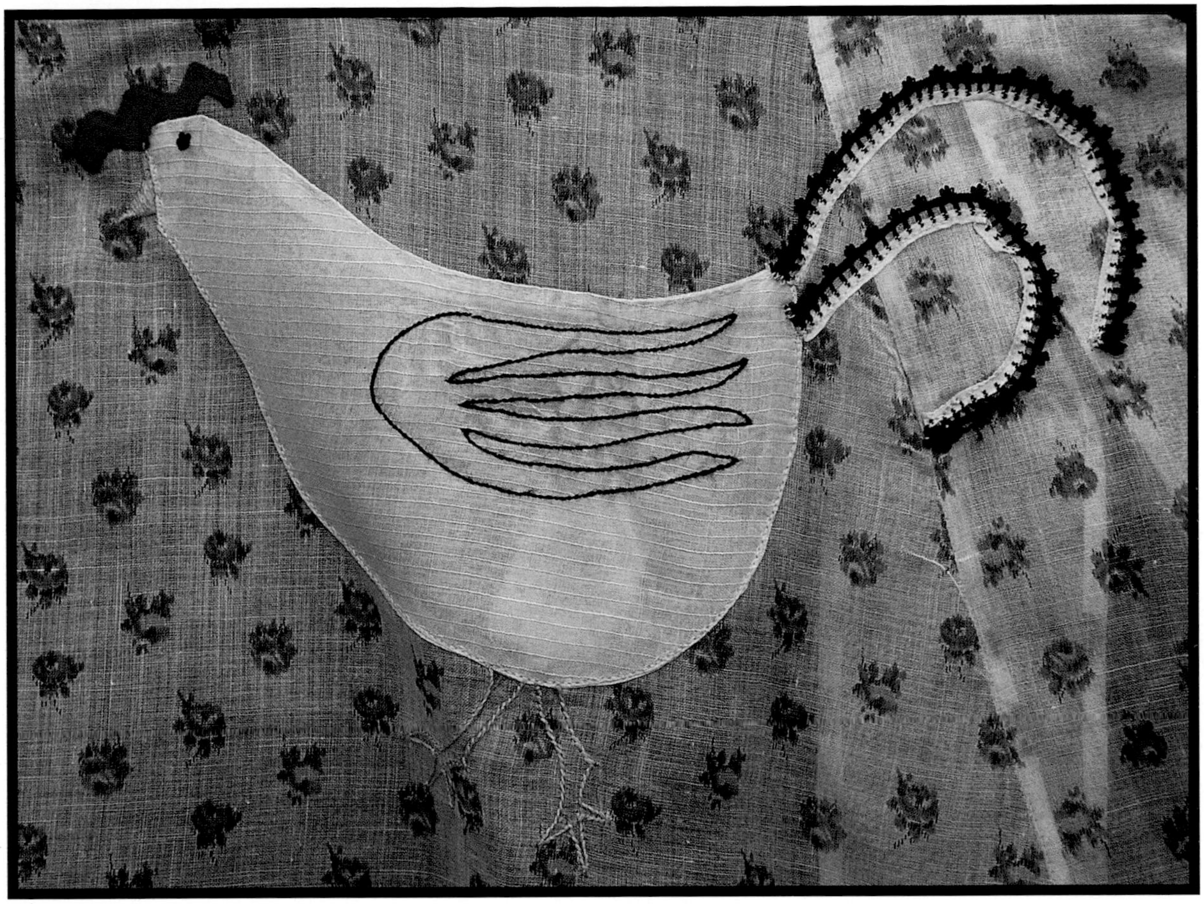

opposite and above: This Fifties organdy apron was made from a pattern that may have appeared in the newspapers, a women's magazine, or a sewing booklet, as aprons of the same style—including the chicken pocket—have been found in many locations. For details, commercial edging and rickrack were combined with hand embroidery.

I cannot abide these apron husbands; such cotqueanes.

—Mistress Gallipot from *The Roaring Girl*
by Thomas Middleton (1580–1627) and Thomas Dekker (1572–1632)
English dramatists

opposite: Sequins make this cotton apron very heavy for everyday wear. Likely it was part of a costume—perhaps for the barn dance scene in a musical. Costumes are difficult to date, as they may be made in one time period to represent another. This apron could have been made as early as the Fifties or as recently as the Nineties.

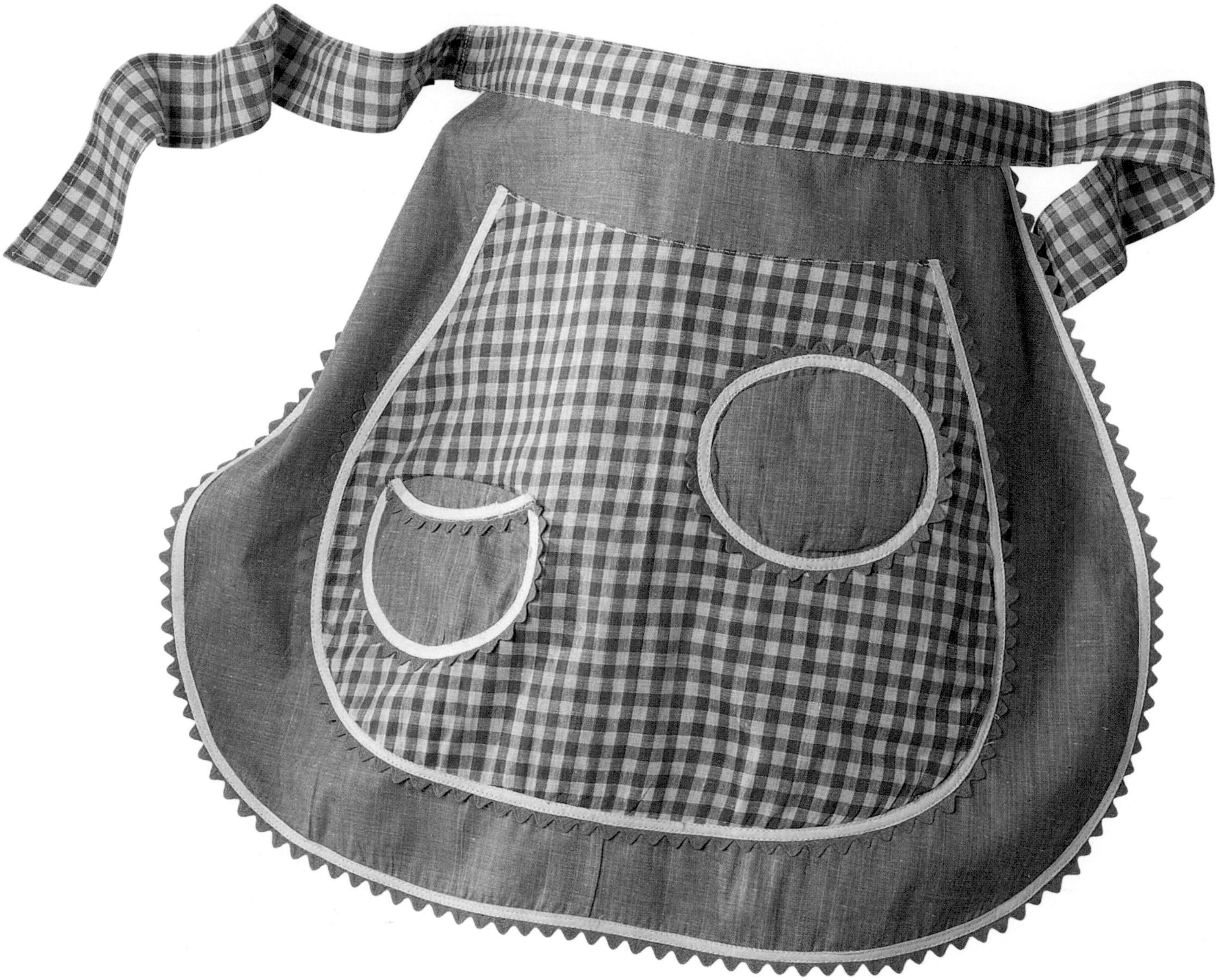

above: The seamstress of this Forties cotton apron attended to details. Borders are edged with three trims—rickrack, bias tape binding, and flat braid, and pockets are padded.
opposite: This Seventies apron-oven mitt set, made from heavy cotton-synthetic blend upholstery fabric, is reminiscent of Ollie from the Sheri Lewis program *Kukla, Fran and Ollie*. Felt, burlap, cotton, and quilt batting are used in the pocket and mitt.

U.S. MARITIME SERVICE
MOTHER

Though they are
now seldom worn,
aprons remain
forever entwined
in our memories.

—Marlene Parkin
American journalist

opposite: This sateen apron with printed pocket was made during World War II.

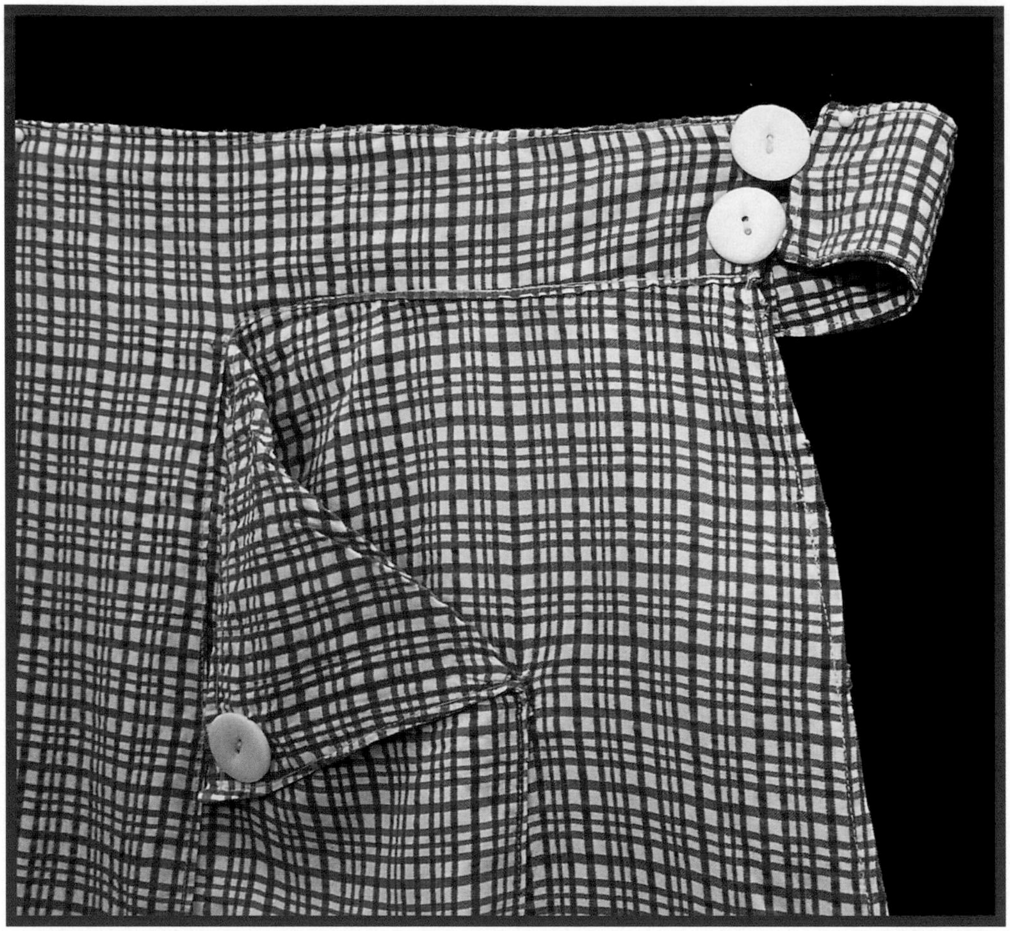

above: This nylon apron with mother-of-pearl buttons is from the late Forties or Fifties.
opposite: This Fifties apron is made of cotton mattress ticking and is decorated with pompoms.

I have always associated aprons with my grandmother, who wore one like a uniform. She made her large wardrobe of

aprons out of scraps

from the work she took in as a seamstress. It seems appropriate to me that, as a young girl, my first sewing project was to make an apron.

—Lucy A. Commoner
Textile Conservator, Smithsonian Institution

opposite: Made from a kit, this Thirties or Forties full apron is decorated with appliqué and embroidery, and is displayed over a commercially made cotton housedress with front zipper closing from the Fifties.

overleaf: Gingham, a lightweight checked cotton, was widely available as early as the Twenties and popular through the Seventies. Rickrack has been available for several decades as well, but reigned supreme in the mid-to late Fifties.

opposite: This is a "pineapple" apron was crocheted in the, Forties or later.

MY LAST WILL AND TESTAMENT.
I, Amy Curtis March, being in my sane mind,
go give and bequeethe all my earthly property—
viz. to wit. . .To my mother, all my clothes,
except the blue apron with pockets—
also my likeness, and my medal, with much love. . . .
I wish my favorite playmate Kitty Bryant
to have the blue silk apron
and my gold-bead ring with a kiss.

—FROM *LITTLE WOMEN*
BY LOUISA MAY ALCOTT
AMERICAN AUTHOR (1832–1888)

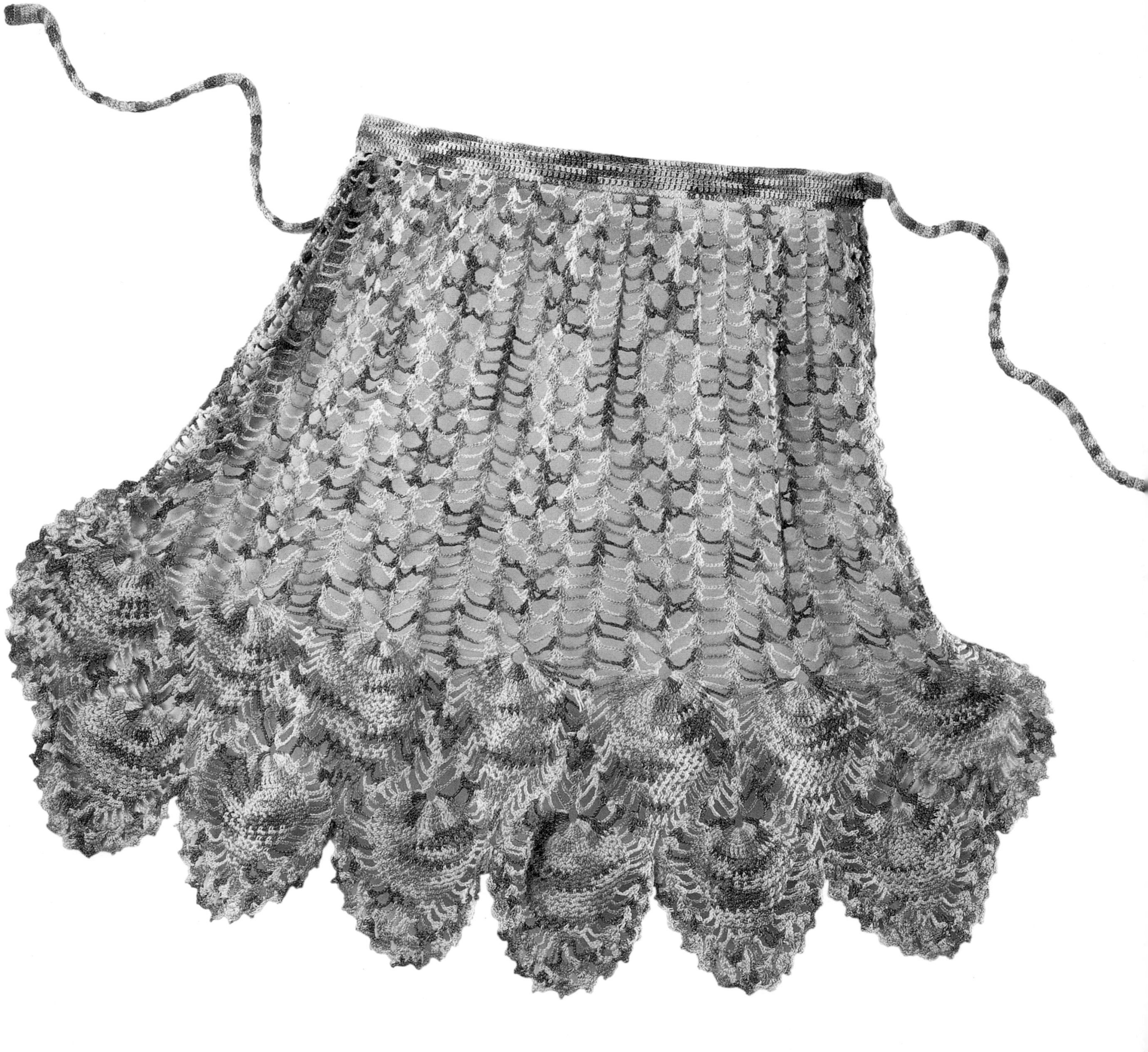

opposite: The print of the fabric itself is the only decoration this Fifties cotton apron needs.

In the kitchen where I grew up there was a drawer for nothing but aprons. My mother and grandmother would not be caught in the kitchen without one. I remember lime green with lace, pink calico, a blue one made from the same material as the tablecloth, a brown one with yellow chickens, a yellow one with tea cups and saucers. The first thing I see when that room rises up in memory is a woman standing by the stove. . . a woman in an apron.

—Anita Skeen
American Author and professor

opposite: The most striking design elements of this starched cotton apron from the Fifties or Sixties are its rich, dark colors. **below:** A Sixties hostess probably wore this apron over black Capri pants. The tulle apron is festooned with peacock feathers, beads, and sequins, each individually sewn to the netting skirt and velveteen ribbon waist.

HOMEMADE STYLES

Until the 1980s most American aprons were handmade at home. For some of these aprons, how they were made is what makes them particularly interesting. The very experience of sewing something from scratch—especially an apron—has a place in our collective history. Most women of baby boomer age and older took Home Economics classes, where making a half apron with a gathered waistband was often the first sewing project: pin the pattern, cut, gather, baste, sew, iron. For a first embroidery project, an apron kit with the pattern printed right on the cloth, or a cross-stitched design on gingham was a smart choice because, in either case, the novice stitcher could "stay in the lines."

The next morning, after breakfast, the green maiden came to fetch Dorothy, and she dressed her in one of the prettiest gowns–made of green brocaded satin. Dorothy put on a green silk apron and tied a green ribbon around Toto's neck, and they started for the Throne Room of the Great Oz.

—FROM *THE WIZARD OF OZ*
BY L. FRANK BAUM (1856–1919)
AMERICAN JOURNALIST, PLAYWRIGHT, AND AUTHOR

opposite: A Forties hostess may have worn this muslin bluebird apron over her sheer cotton dress as she served tea and finger sandwiches to the ladies. No doubt she made her apron from a kit, and she sewed her dress completely by hand.

She wanted to run, breathless as she was, up-stairs to Mr. Linton's room; but I compelled her to sit down on a chair, and made her drink, and washed her pale face, chafing it into a faint colour with my apron.

—Ellen from *Wuthering Heights*
by Emily Brontë (1818–1848)
English novelist

opposite: This handmade smocked gingham apron displayed over a commercially made cotton house dress. Gingham's checked pattern lends itself easily to decorative stitching, and variations of smocking and embroidery abound. Smocking such as this was popular in the Fifties, while cross stitch was popular in the Fifties and into in the early Sixties as well.

above: This apron was a popular summer camp project in the Twenties. Girls learned to cut and assemble the cotton apron and to do the elaborate detailing called cutwork or pullwork. They cut and pulled certain threads, leaving a delicate spider web of threads from the original fabric. They then embellished and reinforced the web by hand-weaving decorative patterns back in with new thread.

opposite: This cotton Fifties apron appears to be a hybrid between homemade and store-bought, in which the whole apron is printed onto a length of fabric, and the seamstress simply cuts it out and hems the edges. Such "apron yard goods" are still available in fabric stores today, often with seasonal, adult, or other novelty themes.

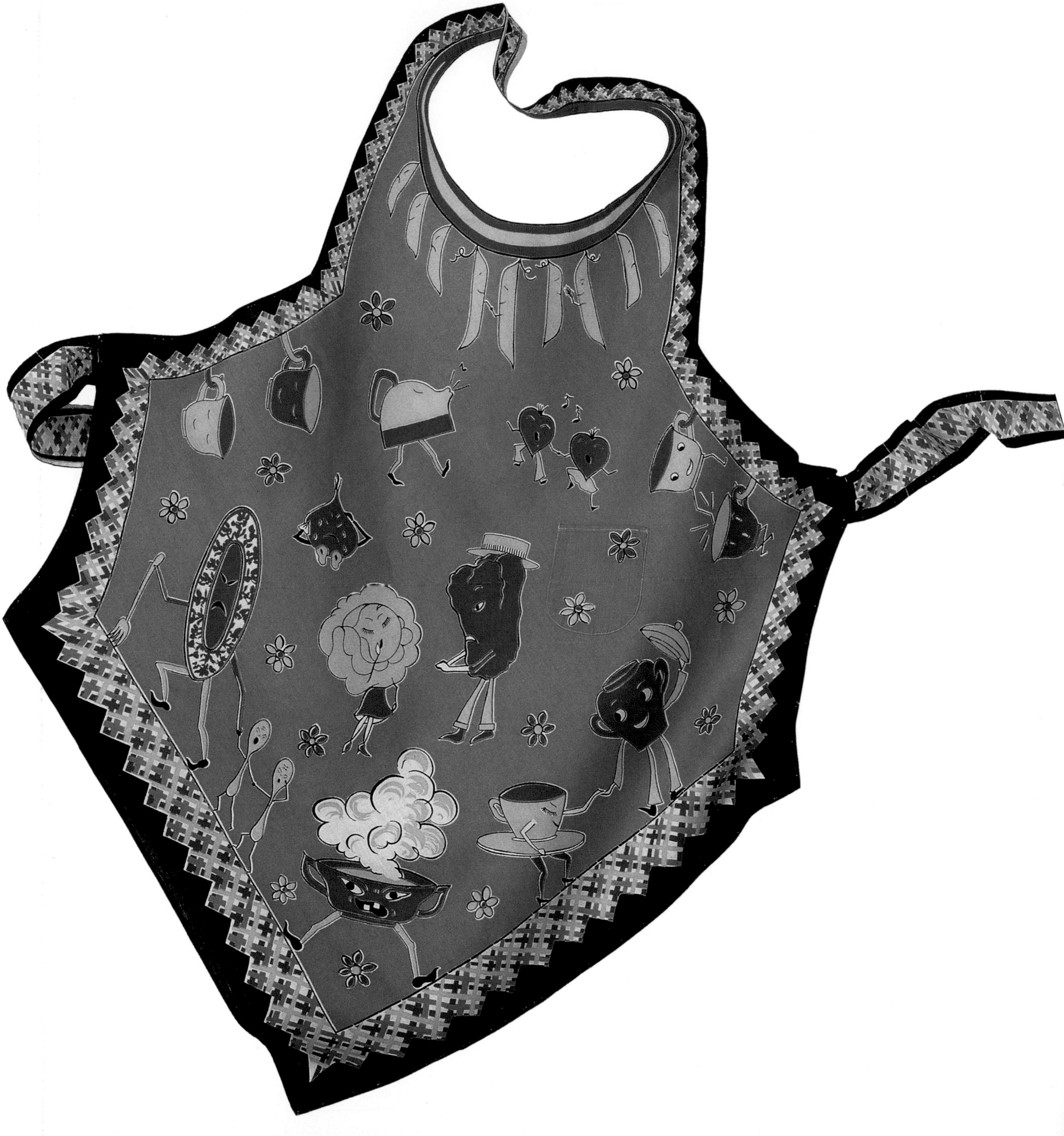

opposite: These two handmade cotton Fifties-early Sixties aprons were found in two different vintage shops in the same city. Although similar in risqué theme, the degree of detail, skill, or sheer patience seem to differ greatly. Perhaps one was made from a kit and the other from scratch. On both the woman's body is hand-painted.

STORE-BOUGHT STYLES

As the mass production of clothing began to release women from their sewing duties (while increasing their need to launder, shop, and earn money), commercially made aprons became widely available, although they were fairly limited in style.

"I'm in sad trouble, Cousin Ribby," said Tabitha, shedding tears. "I've lost my dear son Thomas; I'm afraid the rats have got him." She wiped her eyes with an apron. "He's a bad kitten, Cousin Tabitha; he made a cat's cradle of my best bonnet last time I came to tea."

—Mrs. Tabitha Twitchit from *The Roly-Poly Pudding*
by Beatrix Potter (1866–1943)
English author and illustrator

opposite: Not even the borders of this Sixties cotton synthetic blend apron required stitching. Unhemmed edges were held in place by adhesive in the printed flocking.

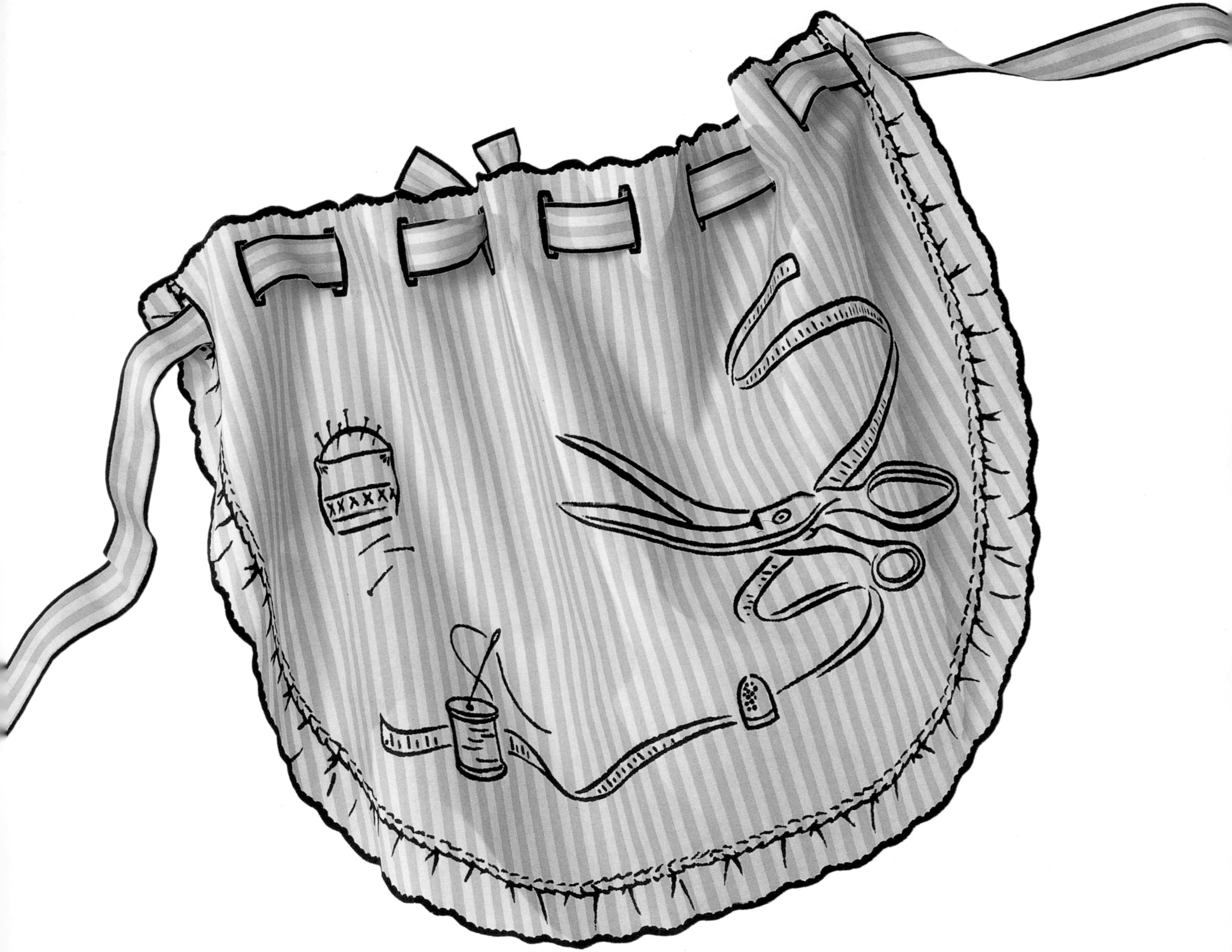

opposite and above: Store-bought cotton aprons with tiny pleats were popular in the Sixties. Manufacturers claimed that the pleats never came out in the wash, but they often did.

Function

WORK APRONS

Some housewives used to say they didn't work. Today we ask parents whether they work *outside* the home, because we know for sure they work *at* home!

For centuries, aprons have protected clothes and wearer while doing messy work. Today, in this age of wash and wear laundry, few of us wear aprons for domestic chores outside of the kitchen, with the exception of canvas nail aprons or leather carpenter's aprons for fix-it chores. In fact, more of us have aprons hanging in the kitchen than actually use them. Still, while some cooks cannot fathom why anyone bothers with aprons, others swear by them.

For work outside the home, some people, such as food handlers and tradespeople still wear aprons for protection. In addition, standardized aprons have emerged as a convenient, inexpensive way to distinguish employees from patrons, and of course, to advertise the store's name.

opposite: With no neck strap, the bib of this cotton waitress apron was held up with pins. Though such pinning was most common early in the century, this apron is from the Forties.

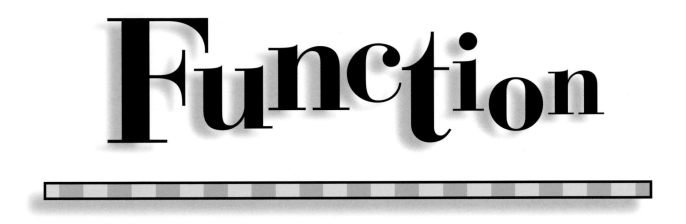

I was 8 years old. . . .
I had visited my relatives often before,
but this was the first time that I
noticed my uncle's apron.
And right away

I took a fancy to this big white apron

with a pocket. . . .
I still remember
how proud I was of my very own apron
and how important I felt to help my uncle with his work.

—Excerpted from a letter that appeared in
My Apron: A Story from My Childhood
by Eric Carle
American Author

upper left: This manufactured nail apron is a style used today by tradespeople, servers, vendors, and anyone else needing handy extra pockets. This particular canvas apron is from the Seventies and was given to lumber-yard customers as a promotion.
upper right: This pockets-only waitress apron, just big enough for order pad, pencil, and tips, is a cotton-polyester blend, suggesting that it is from the Sixties or later.
bottom: This cotton apron was commercially made by a uniform company in a Forties style. Because some restaurants left uniform styles unchanged for decades, and because some have returned to a retro or nostalgic look, this style is hard to date. However, this particular apron's thick cotton fabric says Forties.

RICE LUMBER
Shelburne, Vermont
Phone 802/985-333

below: These hand-made serving aprons from the Twenties are made of very delicate cotton and commercial lace. These aprons required starching and frequent ironing, and were probably worn by domestics in wealthy households, for duties such as serving food.

below: This apron's cut and sturdy blue-and-white checkered fabric were common in the Fifties and Sixties in many hard-work environments such as commercial kitchens, laundries, and hotels. This particular apron saw a lot of action as evinced by stains and by hand-sewn mends done very carefully to prolong the apron's life. One hole is carefully hand-mended with a patch of the same fabric, with the plaids exactly in line.

CEREMONIAL AND SYMBOLIC APRONS

Special aprons play a part in traditional customs, ceremonies, and costumes worldwide. Such attire may announce to others the locale, religion, group affiliation, or position of the wearer. Fashions in aprons, headwear, hairstyle, jewelry, or other items broadcast women's sexual status in terms of virginity, fertility, marriage, or parenthood. In the United States, some decorative aprons seem to advertise the wearer's sexuality and serve as seductive accessory; just think of what the French Maid costume represents. More commonly, though, decorative aprons reflected economic status simply through the fact that the wearer had the materials, skills, and lifestyle to craft and wear an apron designed for show rather than work.

If ceremonial aprons are defined as those reserved only for certain special occasions, then holiday aprons are the closest we come to ceremonial aprons in the mainstream United States. Even today, it's a good guess that if you've got just one special apron, it's for a holiday.

One Slavic wedding tradition involved capping, in which bridesmaids circled the bride and sang songs mourning the loss of her childhood as they coiled her long hair and tucked it into a cap which the married woman could never again remove in public. That ritual has evolved in some U.S. immigrant communities to one in which the bridesmaids, singing a mix of mournful and romantic songs, remove the bride's veil and tie on an apron.

opposite: The convertible apron-bonnet, a novelty in the Fifties, was made of lightweight cotton for cool sun protection yet sturdy carrying capacity. The blue apron-bonnet shown was probably given as a gift, as it had this handwritten verse in its pocket:
I'm an apron you can see
Button me up, I'm a bonnet cute as can be.

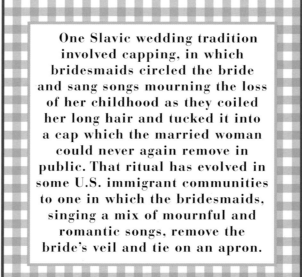

The apron is one of the most basic forms of clothing. . . . It draws symbolic and magic power from the sex to which it both calls attention and provides modesty and protective cover. . . . much of [apron language and lore] has to do with sexuality, fertility, and marital relations and testifies to the significance of the apron's position on the body.

—BETH ALBERTY

CURATOR OF "APROPOS APRON," METROPOLITAN MUSEUM OF ART

above: Until recent decades, women and girls of the Kirdi tribe in Cameroon, West Africa have worn short beaded aprons called *cache sexes* (French for "to cover one's sex"). Traditionally, the husband cut the apron's lower edge on the couple's wedding night to symbolize the bride's loss of virginity. This 9- by 16-inch apron features beads, string, and shells.

opposite: For special occasions, Hmong women of Northern Thailand don colorful embroidered and appliquéd aprons with long red, pink, or orange sashes that wrap around the waist, and long tassels that tie and hang down the back. This apron is a traditional style that's still worn today. Each tie is 7½ feet long.

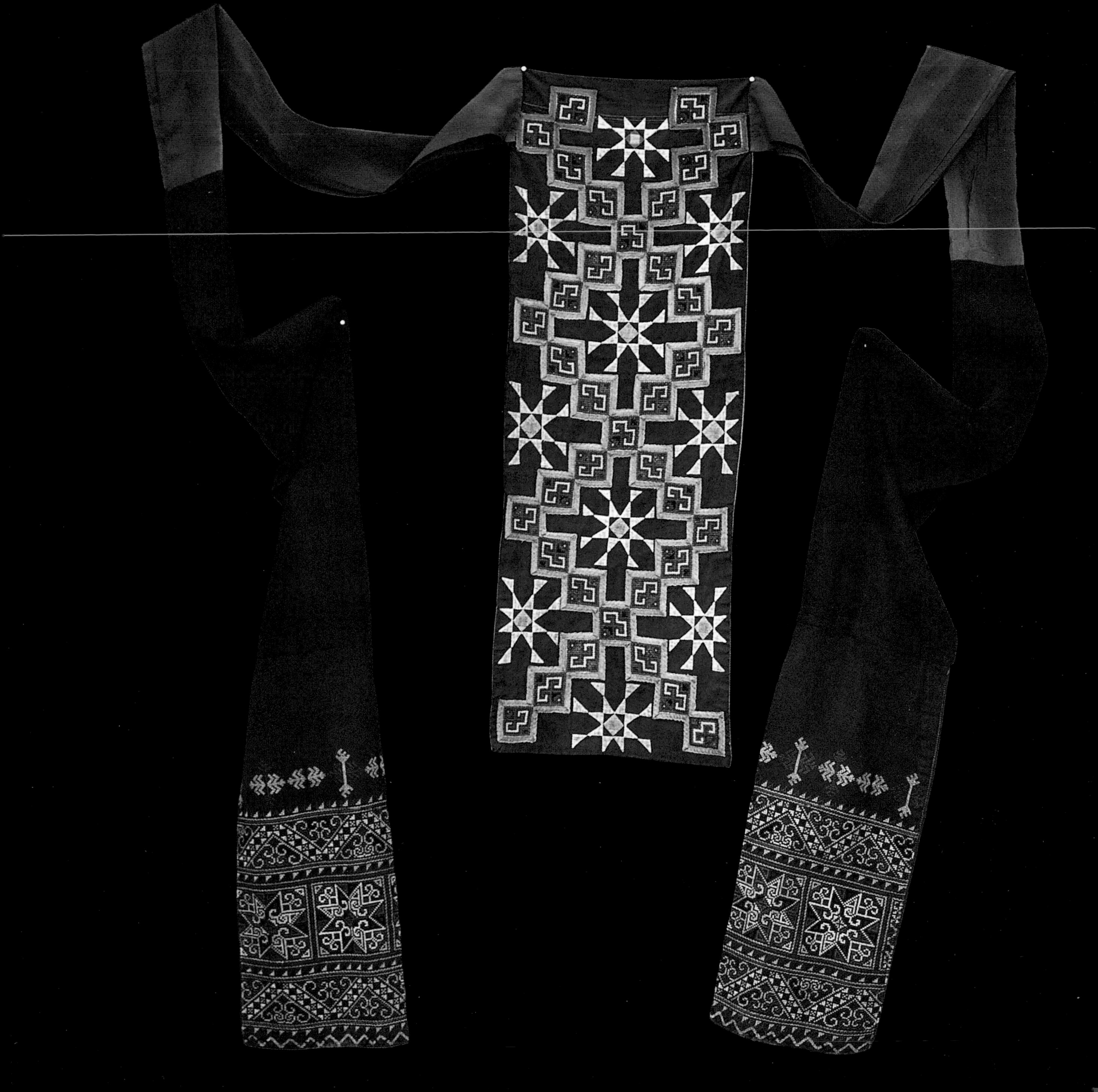

back: This organdy hostess apron found in various color combinations, was made from a popular Fifties pattern. The flowers were made by hand-crocheting rickrack into chains of blossoms.
front: The accent colors of this organdy hostess apron, chartreuse and pink, were popular in the Fifties. The apron was designed to be folded up and ironed all at once.

Her binding proceeds with clock-like monotony. . . .
At intervals she stands up to rest, and to retie her disarranged
apron, or to pull her bonnet straight. Then one can see the
oval face of a handsome young woman with deep dark eyes and long
heavy clinging tresses, which seem to clasp in a beseeching way
anything they fall against. The cheeks are paler, the teeth more
regular, the red lips thinner than is usual in a country-bred girl.
It is Tess Durbeyfield, otherwise d'Urberville . . .

—FROM *TESS OF THE D'URBERVILLES*
BY THOMAS HARDY (1840-1928)
ENGLISH NOVELIST AND POET

A n apron is simply a loin cloth with ruffles.

—Gloria D. Nixon-John
Director, Oakland (CA) Writing Project

opposite: This late Forties ensemble consists of a handmade sheer starched organdy pinafore with rickrack-edged ruffles worn over a commercially-made rayon dress.

opposite: This Fifties hostess apron of netting, polished cotton, and metallic rickrack was probably made to be worn with one specific dress.

Mom wore a practical apron in the kitchen, but right before she entered the dining room to serve her guests, she traded her no-nonsense apron for a fancy one, sewn to match her outfit, a holiday theme, or even the placemats! Many such aprons were gifts; for example, from guest to hostess, from bride to the women in the wedding party, or from the church supper organizer to the volunteer servers and cooks. Netting or other sheer fabric was often used when making matching gift aprons for a group. Unlike opaque aprons, which could hide a multitude of sewing sins on the back, sheer aprons left no room for sloppiness or mistakes as all the cutting and stitching would show through.

Merry Christmas
Merry Christmas

Some good matronly woman in a pork-pie hat

to mother him.

Take him in tow, platter face and a large apron.

—FROM *ULYSSES*
BY JAMES JOYCE (1882-1941)
IRISH NOVELIST, SHORT-STORY WRITER, AND POET

opposite: This cotton apron belonged to a woman who wore it for many years through the middle decades of the century, but only to serve Thanksgiving dinner.

Previous Overleaf

lower left: The seamstress who made this organdy apron was probably experimenting with her new machine's zigzag feature. The apron is simply a rectangle, gathered by placing a waistband through a casing along the top, a style that lasted only a short time in the Fifties because it was uncomfortable.

upper left: This Fifties burlap apron, lined with cotton and accented with ribbon, felt, sequins, and beads, is cut to cover a full skirt.

center: Judging from the fabric and style, this white polyester apron is from the Seventies or later.

lower right: This Nineties apron is made of sheer cotton, but it appears almost opaque because it is layered. Handmade Christmas aprons are still made and sold at craft fairs and church bazaars so they can be hard to date.

upper right: Cotton border prints were popular in the Fifties and Sixties.

NOVELTY APRONS

Commercially made aprons with printed words that let wearers have their say started showing up in the Fifties and are still being made today. Some remind women of what we're supposed to do, and others give us a chance to say how we feel about it. Text apron themes commonly available today (besides advertising) include female spunk ("You don't like my cooking, get outta my kitchen"), aging ("I may be an oldie but I'm a goodie"), flirtation ("Kiss the cook"), and the irony of the highly-educated homemaker ("I learned this in college").

Souvenir aprons were also popular in the Fifties—replaced today by T-shirts with pithy sayings like: "They went to the Bahamas and all I got was this stupid T-shirt." Many world travelers have returned home with "authentic native" aprons, sometimes true to tradition but more commonly, adulterated in style or fabric. If you find an "authentic native apron" from Brazil, for example, check for a "Made in China" label and do a little research to see whether traditional Brazilian garb actually includes aprons.

. . . Fitzroy wooing her so closely that really he did seem *tied* to her apron strings.

—FROM *A PERILOUS SECRET*
BY CHARLES READE (1814–1884)
ENGLISH NOVELIST

opposite: This commercially made apron explains "How to Keep Your Husband" in both French and English: Don't be jealous; Don't sulk; Kiss him often; If he's tired bring him his favorite drink; Show him you love him; No gossip over the phone; Don't read his mail; Don't ever get mad; Don't take a superior attitude; Always look innocent; Let him read his paper in peace; Watch your weight.

DO
DON'T
HOW TO KEEP YOUR HUSBAND
Always look innocent!
Ayez toujours l'air innocente!
Show him you love him
Montrez-lui que vous l'aimez
Let him read his paper in peace
Laissez-le lire son journal en paix.
Kiss him often!
Embrassez-le souvent!
Watch your weight!
Attention à votre poids!
If he is tired bring him his favorite drink
S'il est fatigué, servez-lui sa boisson favorite.
Don't ever get mad!
Ne vous mettez jamais en colère!
No gossip over the phone.
Pas de commérages au téléphone.
Don't sulk!
Ne boudez pas!
Don't read his mail.
Ne lisez pas son courrier.
Don't be jealous!

HER MAJESTY
Queen of the Kitchen

Aprons are among the most important cultural markers of women's lives—intersecting their selves and connecting them with each other. While they evoke women's caring roles as nurturers, these simple, functional objects are also symbols of a profound social ambivalence about our expectations of women—to the degree that "apron strings" tie unwilling women to the home and restless children to binding relationships. Yet people need to be fed and feeding people involves making a mess. Hence, the need for aprons. The variety of aprons illustrates the ways in which women have made this cultural assignment a means of individual self-expression and identity.

—Dorothy C. Miller
American Author and Professor

opposite: Note Capri pants worn by "Queen of the Kitchen" on this commercially made apron. Terry cloth aprons became popular in the Sixties.

One popular Fifties tourist apron showed a woman holding a bottle and leaning on a lamppost, with hairdo and party dress askew. The caption read, "To Hell with housework. Let's go to New Orleans."

opposite: Souvenir state aprons such as this one were common in the Fifties, with the geography of the maps printed on them freely altered to accentuate popular locations.

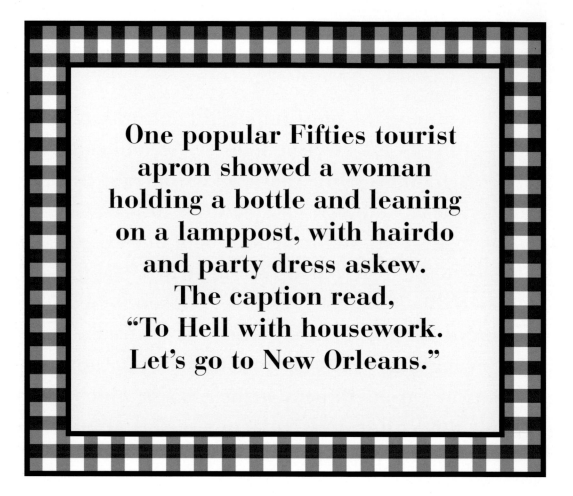

WYOMING
SHERIDAN
LOVELL
CODY
GREYBULL
BASIN
SUNDANCE
MOORCROFT
BLACK HILLS
NEWCASTLE
TEAPOT DOME
WORLAND
THERMOPOLIS
HELL'S HALF ACRE
LANCE CREEK
GRAND TETON NAT. PARK
JENNY LAKE
JACKSON
WORLDS LARGEST ELK HERD
Buffalo Bills Home
OLD FAITHFUL
SHOSHONI
RIVERTON
HUDSON
LANDER
DOUGLAS
LUSK
FORT LARAMIE
TORRINGTON
WHEATLAND
CHUGWATER
WORLD'S GREATEST FOSSIL FISH BEDS
MEDICINE BOW
RAWLINS
ROCK RIVER
STATE CAPITOL
KEMMERER
GRANGER
ROCK SPRINGS
GREEN RIVER
EVANSTON
OLD FORT BRIDGER
STATE UNIVERSITY
LARAMIE
CHEYENNE
PINE BLUFF
GRAND TETON NAT. PARK

Mama worked for private
families most of her life,
cleaning, ironing, cooking,
and serving parties.

When she served she wore a white uniform,

but she always
spruced it up with
a colorful apron.

—Patricia C. McKissack
American Author

opposite: This apron is an example of pieced cotton textile work by the Seminole American Indians of Florida. It is a typical tourist apron in that it's partly authentic: The piecing is traditional, but aprons are not part of traditional Seminole garb.

CHILDREN'S APRONS

Children's aprons are often real gems because many were handmade with loving care for one special child. Mother–daughter matching aprons were popular, and if there was a scrap left over, maybe the doll got a matching apron as well. Lots of girls and boys wore aprons and smocks for serious culinary or artistic pursuits. If you ever painted at an easel in kindergarten, you probably wore a smock, which was as much like a shirt worn backwards as an apron.

It's hard to find children's aprons at thrift store or rummage sales; either people save them for sentimental reasons, or kids just run them into the ground. If you do find one, no doubt you'll see evidence of the love sewn into it and reminisce about the cover-ups you once wore—the barbecue apron that was just your size and embroidered with your name, the ruffled pinafore for dress-up, the plain pinafore from your school uniform, or a very short pinafore or "pinnie" to identify your team in gym class. Remember wearing a grown-up half-apron tied up under your armpits so it wouldn't drag on the floor or one of Dad's shirts switched around with the buttons in back and the sleeves all rolled up?

Grettel shook out her apron so that the pearls and precious stones rolled about the room, and Hansel threw down one handful after the other out of his pocket. Thus all their troubles were ended, and they lived happily ever afterward.

—FROM *THE FAIRY TALE BOOKS*, "HANSEL AND GRETTEL"
BY ANDREW LANG (1844-1912)
SCOTTISH SCHOLAR AND MAN OF LETTERS

left: This child-sized plaid cotton bib apron with large pockets could be from the Fifties, Sixties, or Seventies.
right: The Brownie Scout logos on this Fifties cotton apron are hand drawn with fabric markers.
bottom: This toddler's bibbed tool apron has compartments for a whole box of crayons, plus other essentials. Made of cotton-polyester blend, it is from the Seventies or later.

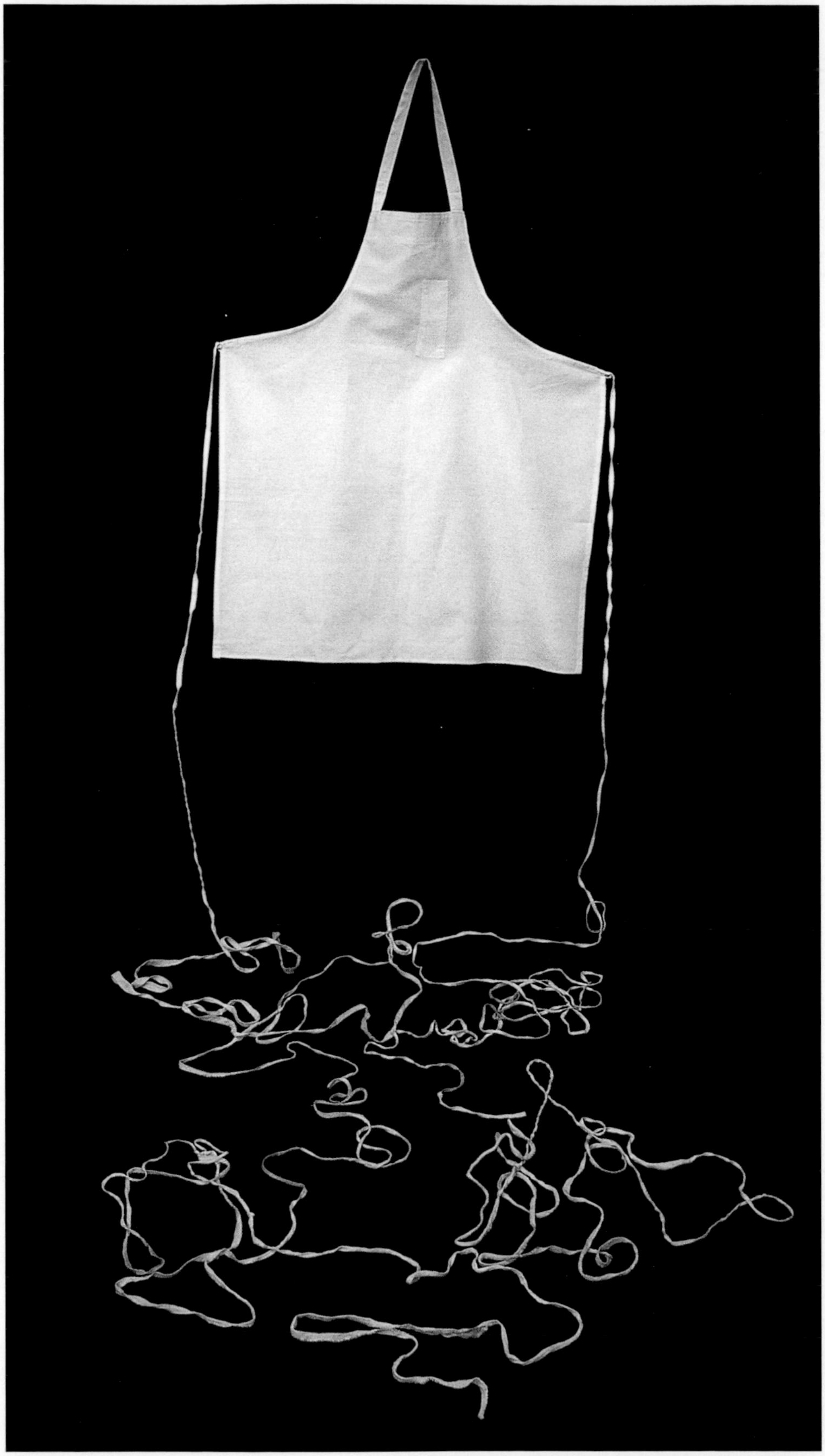

OBJETS D'ART

For decades, painters, sculptors, cartoonists and other artists have used aprons as a symbol to represent family; specifically, housewives and mothers. Scan your art history book and this week's Sunday comics for aprons, or watch on stage at the theater. For example, in a recent children's play, the audience knew that the dinosaur wearing the apron was Mom. Or, in an adult solo dance performance, the dancer in black leotards transformed from character to character; we recognized Mom by the apron.

Clearly many artists recognize the strength of aprons as symbols. Bonnie Stone (California) and others depicted their life stories on aprons for a group show. Marie Samuel (Illinois) included aprons in several of her quilted statements on women's lives. Miriam Schaer (New York) produced "Rules of Engagement," a series of aprons with images of idealized women and quotes from Sun Tsu's *The Art of War*. Florence Alfano McEwin (Wyoming) beaded a tiny apron, "For Josephine Baker When it's too Hot to Wear Anything Else." Ellen Rulseh (Wisconsin) presented a solo show, "Having a Say, An Exhibition of Aprons and Voices", in which she portrayed twenty characters inspired by thrift store aprons. Marcie Stoyke-Riley (Minnesota) produced a video documentary called *Women and Their Aprons*, in which several women display special aprons and explain their significance.

The contemporary aprons shown here are works created by professional artists. Each was designed for an invitational theme exhibition in 1996, and was constructed from a basic white canvas butcher's apron.

Among the objects we take for granted in our kitchens, the apron ranks somewhere along with teacups and scissors.

—Theresa Bedal
American Journalist

opposite: "Snarl," Andrea Fuhrman, 1996. Standard commercial butcher/chef apron, of lightweight canvas, cotton cloth tape. Fuhrman is an artist and an educator.

There was a pretty woman at the back of the shop,

dancing a little child in her arms,

while another little fellow

clung to her apron.

—FROM *DAVID COPPERFIELD*
BY CHARLES DICKENS (1812-1870)
ENGLISH NOVELIST

opposite: "Mom's Diner," Sarah Linquist, 1996. Airbrushed and stenciled in a Thirties style on a standard commercial butcher/chef apron. Linquist is mother of two and partner in On the Wall Productions, creators of fine art playthings such as inflatable versions of Munch's "The Scream," a working Salvidor Dali-esque melted clock, and a Pin-the-Ear-on-Van Gogh game.

MOM'S
DINER
NOT A DRIVE THRU!
Linquist '96

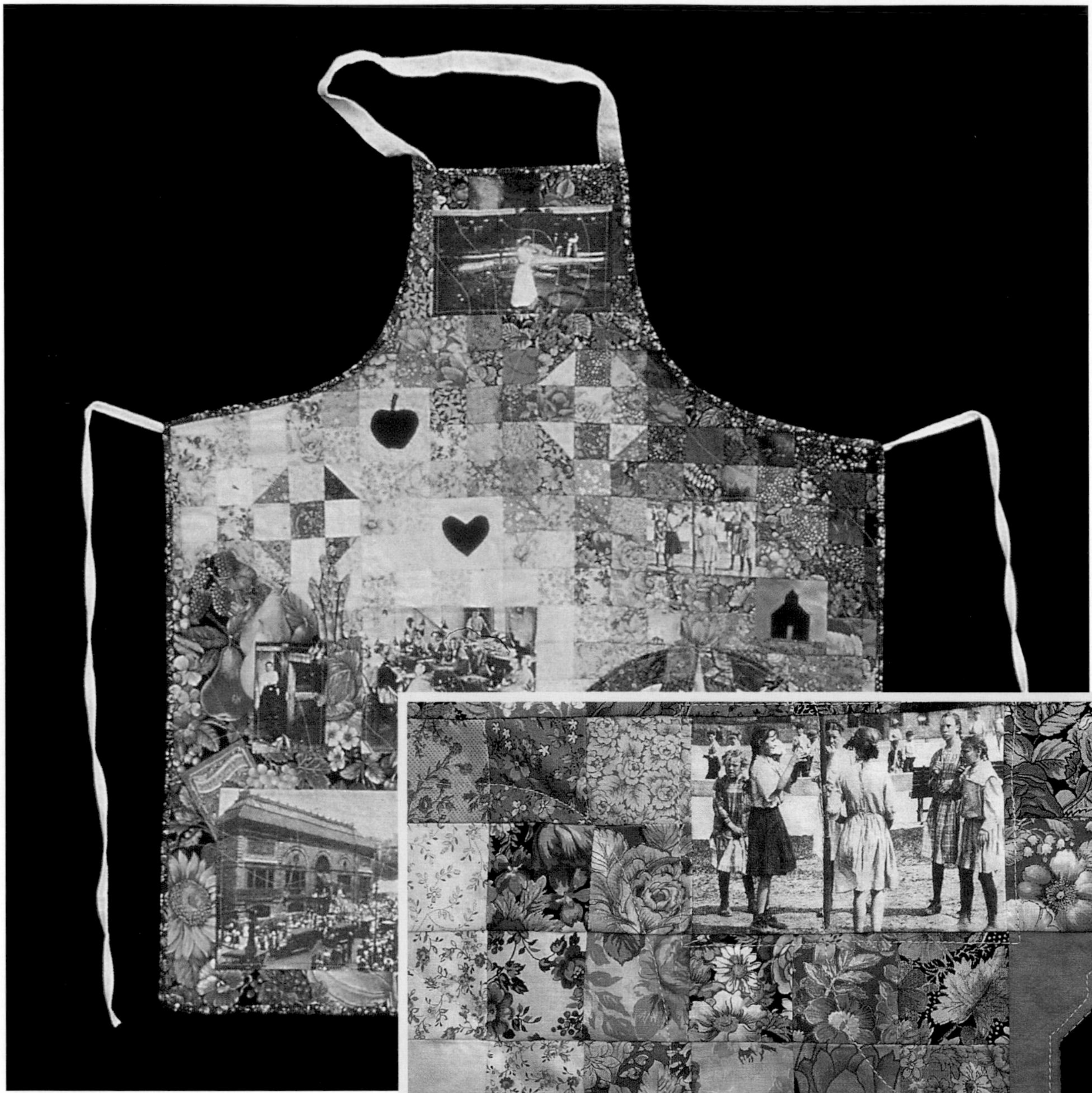

opposite: "Remembering Our Herstory," Sister Josephine Neimann, School Sisters of Notre Dame, 1996. Standard commercial butcher/chef apron of lightweight canvas with quilting, appliqué, and cyanotype photos depicting early Twentieth-century street scenes and factory scene, women's suffrage rally circa 1917, woman in chicken yard. Neimann explained why she included the chicken yard photo: "My mother raised chickens and could keep the money to spend as she wished. One small step to freedom."

"We did set him free—me and Tom. . . . we had to steal candles, and the sheet, and the shirt, and your dress, and spoons, and tin plates, and case-knives, and the warming-pan, and the grindstone, and flour, and just no end of things, and you can't think what work it was to make the saws, and pens, and inscriptions, and one thing or another . . . and get up and down the lightning-rod, and dig the hole into the cabin, and made the rope ladder and send it in cooked up in a pie, and send in spoons and things to work with in your apron pocket—"

—Huck from *The Adventures of Huckleberry Finn*
by Mark Twain (1835-1910)
American humorist, newspaperman, lecturer, and writer

opposite: "Ma Che Carini, or Good Enough to Eat," Kathryn Adamchick, 1996. "Ma che carini" in Italian, means "my, what little dears." The phrase evolved to "maccheroni" or, in American, "macaroni." Cotton apron, pasta in various shapes including wheels, bow ties, elbows, and some X-rated body parts. Adamchick is an artist, art educator, and curator.

He heard the rustle of the apron.

—FROM *SONS AND LOVERS*
BY D.H. LAWRENCE (1885–1930)
ENGLISH NOVELIST, SHORT-STORY WRITER, POET, AND ESSAYIST

EAT

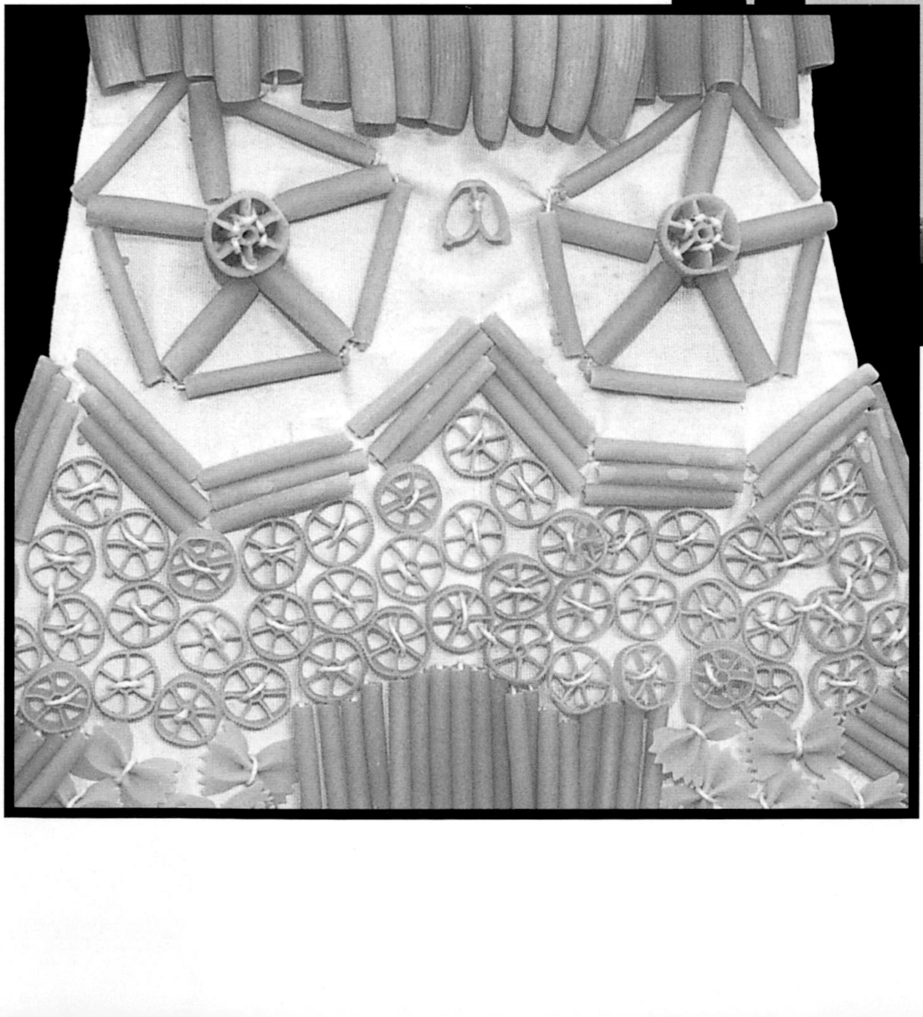

The guys, they pulled a fast one on us. . . .
Most women these days work two full time jobs:
one at the office and the other at home.
Sure, it's great that we cracked the glass ceiling.
Women are more empowered than ever—
a victory that is not to be diminished,
within a war that still goes on.
But now it's time to

take the power

we've fought so hard for and put it to work
—on the homefront.
Men need to start picking up the slack. . . .
Our aim is to help you cinch those apron strings
tight around your husband's waist,
and to keep him tethered
to the spatula, mop, and vacuum—
his new after-work buddies—
whether he likes them or not.

–KERI PENTAUK
AMERICAN JOURNALIST

opposite: "Warm Milk," Lynnie McElwee, 1996. This apron's skirt has two layers: the top is pink gingham with ruffles; underneath is a dark red appliquéd and embroidered hearth with a "fire" roaring in it. Standard commercial butcher/chef apron of light-weight canvas, synthetic bird's nest and birds, beads, mixed media. Says the artist, "Creating this apron was both a creative and an engineering challenge." McElwee is an artist and teaches visual art to deaf children.

Unfolding an Apron's History

Most aprons become meaningful because of the stories they tell, the eras they represent, and the feelings they evoke in us. To discover the stories in the aprons you own or may acquire, you can start by determining the age of the apron. If you know the maker or owner, ask when it was sewn and what sort of chores or occasions it was used for. If you don't know who owned the apron, sleuthing its history will be a more complex endeavor, as apron dating is both art and science. Here are some ways that you may find useful. . .

• USE OLD PICTURES AS GUIDES

Look through old magazines, newspapers, catalogs, or patterns to find aprons like yours. Then, you can assume your apron is the same vintage as the publication.

above: This ankle-length apron is of a style common in the late nineteenth century. The waist is small to accommodate corseting. Materials include silk satin, silk cording, cotton lining.

• IDENTIFY THE SHAPE OR STYLE WITH AN ERA

Look at the apron's shape. What dress style is the apron designed to cover—long, short, full, close-fitting? Once you've determined dress shape, look for pictures of vintage clothing to identify your apron's decade.

Their supper was the feast of two girls. Carol was in the dining-room, in a frock of black satin edged with gold, and Bea, in blue gingham and an apron, dined in the kitchen; but the door was open between. . . .

—FROM *MAIN STREET*
BY SINCLAIR LEWIS (1885-1951)
AMERICAN NOVELIST

opposite: This ankle-length turn-of-the-century apron is hand sewn of silk fabric, cotton lining, and commercial lace. The apron is designed to fit a woman with a small waist and ample bust, made fashionable through corseting. Full-length aprons with pinned bibs—no neck straps—were common early in the century. They were made occasionally into the Fifties and are still worn today by Amish women.

above: These aprons are from the turn of the century as revealed by their length (to the ankle) and by their fabric width. Note that both aprons are made of more than one width of fabric sewn together. In Victorian times cloth was woven only 24–28 inches wide, so seamstresses had to combine multiple widths of cloth.

above left: The print apron was probably for dress as it shows little wear. It is unusual as most turn-of-the-century aprons were solid white.

above right: The white apron was definitely for dressy occasions, as the lace is handmade and of excellent quality.

• STUDY THE FABRIC ITSELF

Look to see what type of cloth it is—natural fiber, synthetic, or a blend. Find out when the material was first available and when it had been in style. Also inspect how the cloth is woven, and when that width or technique was used or popular.

• INSPECT THE STITCHING

Find out when the type of stitching on your apron was available. The first commercial machines had one-thread chain stitching, so a snag could unravel that whole seam. Later, machines progressed to two-thread interlocking bobbin-and-needle seams. Zigzag machines were first sold to homemakers in the late Fifties.

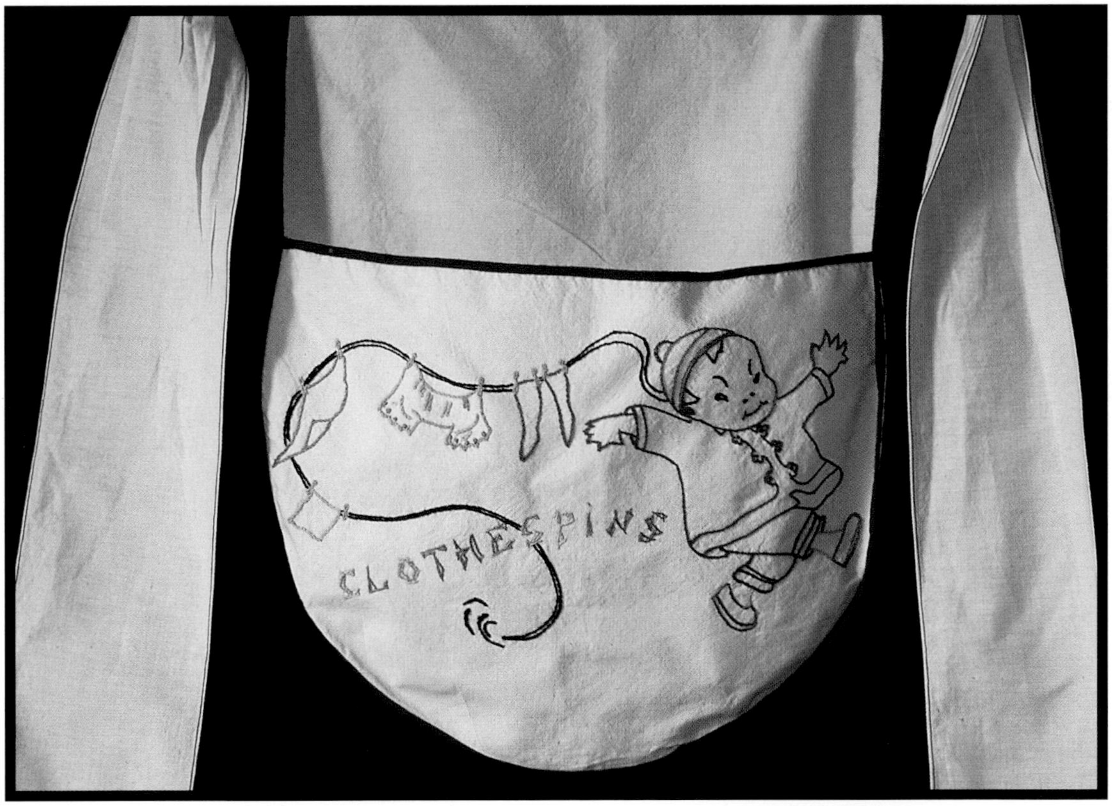

above: The embroidered cotton apron was made from a kit in the Forties or Fifties, and was meant to be worn as a clothespin carrier by laundresses hanging wash on the line.

• EXAMINE THE DECORATION

What techniques and materials are used for embellishment? When were they in vogue? For example, embroidery was popular from Victorian times through the Twenties (as women stitched to demonstrate their feminine skills), embroidered apron kits became available in the Twenties, and cross-stitch embroidery was common in the Fifties and Sixties.

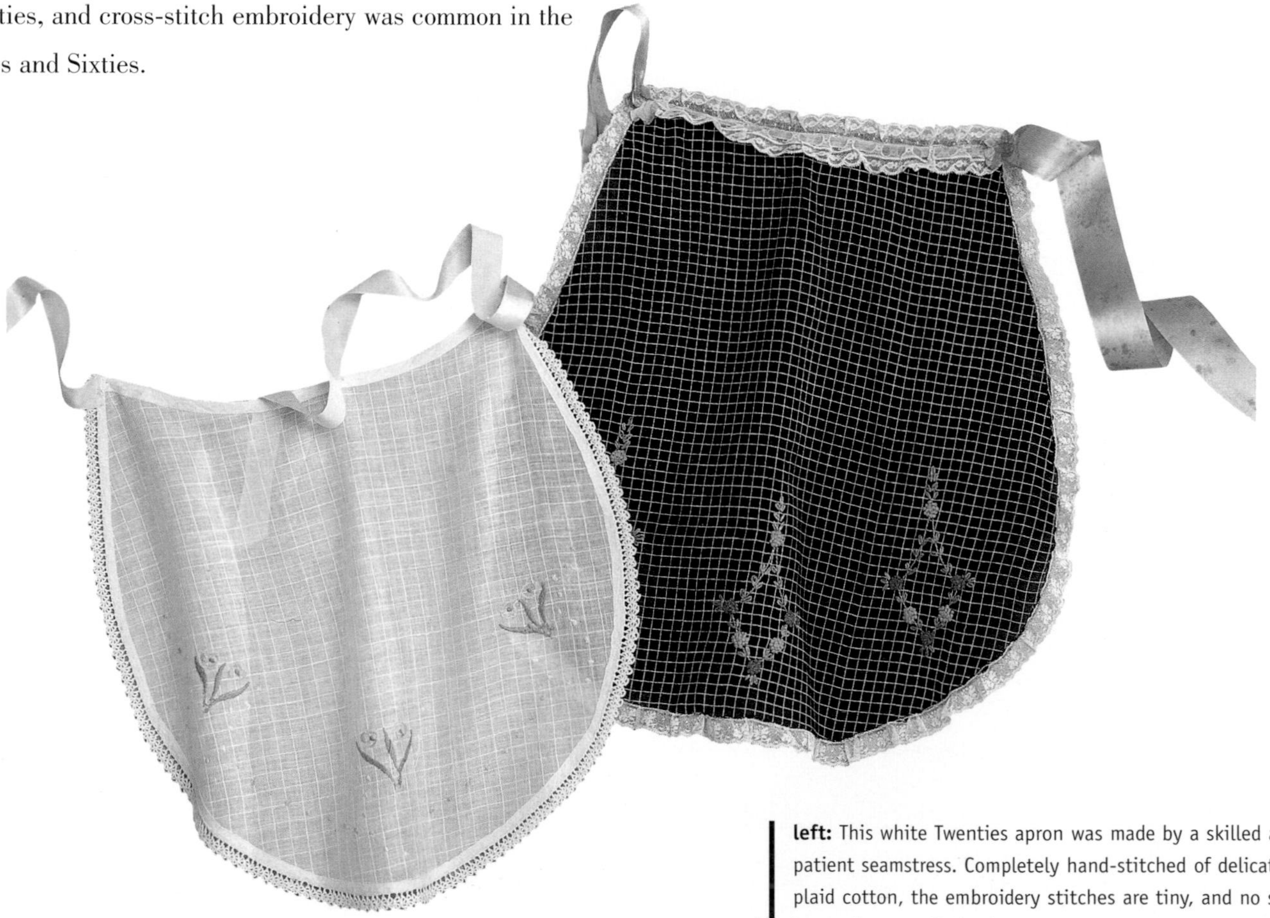

left: This white Twenties apron was made by a skilled and patient seamstress. Completely hand-stitched of delicate window plaid cotton, the embroidery stitches are tiny, and no strings or knots show on the back.
right: This black Twenties apron was hand sewn and embroidered, with commercial trim attached with hand stitching.

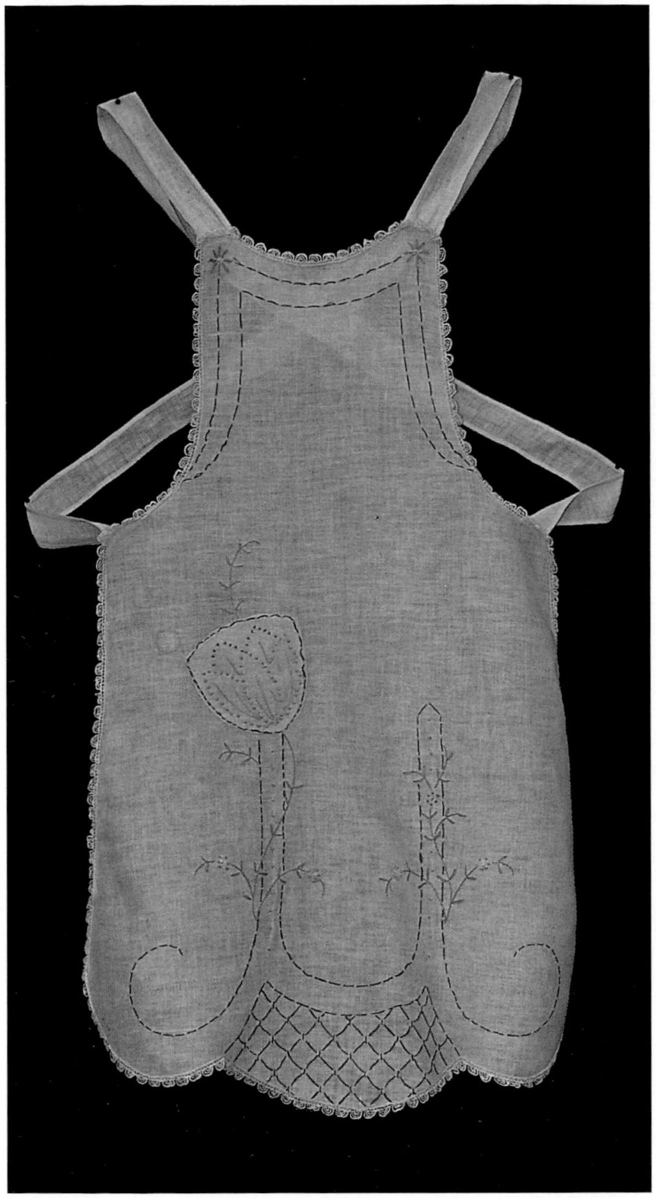

above and right: This full apron, typical of the Twenties, is very well made. The sheer cotton body has careful hand embroidery, and is edged with commercial lace attached with hand stitching.

• NOTE THE COLORS

Colors pass in and out of fashion. For example, from the turn of the century through the Twenties, white aprons were worn by domestics for serving food to guests. In the Thirties, garment colors in general were muted. In the post-war Forties, garment colors were becoming more vibrant, and by the Fifties, bright colors were fair game. Chartreuse was popular as were pink-and-black combinations. In the Sixties and Seventies, turquoise, harvest gold, and avocado green and brown were popular colors.

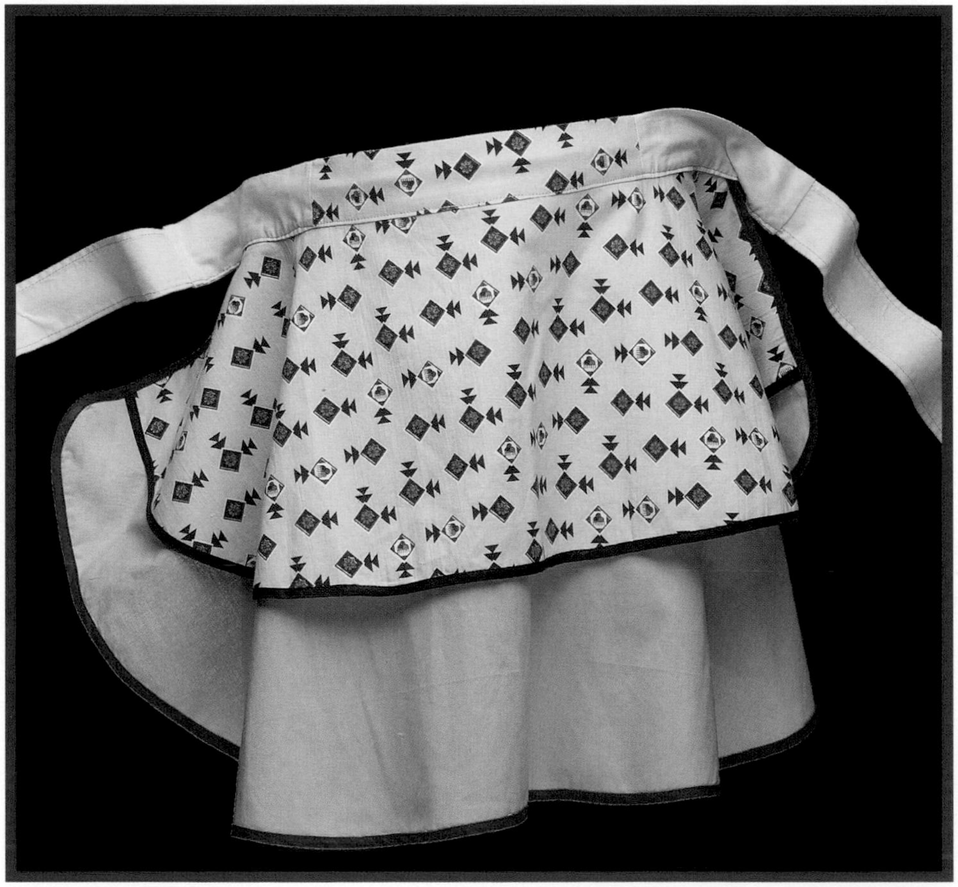

above: This Fifties reversible chartreuse cotton apron is an inventive use of fabric remnants.

above: This apron has two clues relating to era: shape and color. The flared shape fits over a Fifties full skirt, and pink and black were popular in the Fifties. The seamstress had a good eye for design when she selected a swirling print and rounded pocket shape to accent the swing of the full skirt.

• LOOK FOR PRINTED FASHION AND DESIGN CLUES

If the fabric has a printed picture, check hairdos, clothes, appliances, and furniture for clues to help you identify the era.

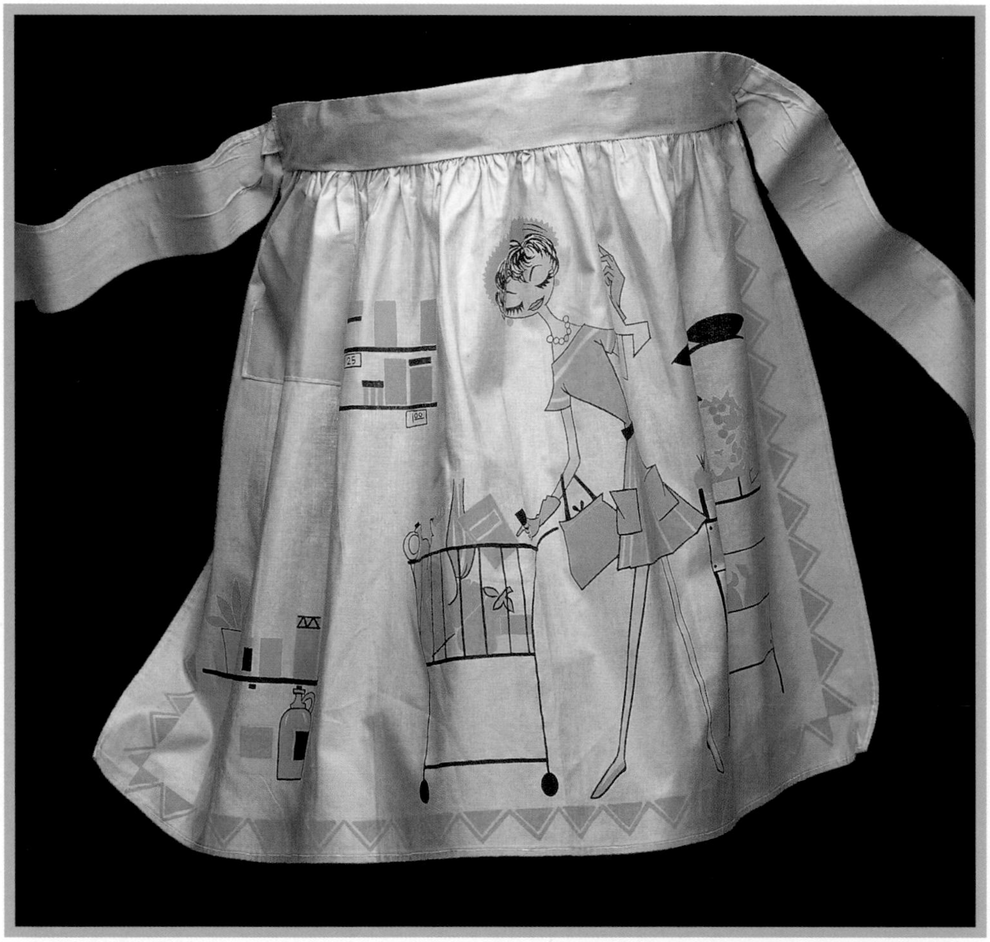

above: This commercially made polished cotton apron is from the early Sixties. Note the shopper's pearls, the hat tilted back on her head, the pink and turquoise colors, and the sleek cut of her clothes. Think Jackie Kennedy.

• DRAW FROM YOUR GENERAL KNOWLEDGE OF HISTORY

If you found a souvenir apron printed with a map of the state of Alaska, you would probably figure out pretty quickly that that it couldn't have been made earlier than 1959 (the year Alaska became the 49th state of the Union); or if you found an apron with a border print of Volkswagen Bugs, you could guess that it was made after World War II. Such clues can give you a starting point for further research.

below: This Forties World War II USO uniform displays a "V for Victory" in Morse code. The United Services Organization was a civilian non-profit organization serving the military and their families.

above: "Matching undies" aprons such as these were made and given as gifts in the Seventies, and paisley was a common print of that decade.

•CONSIDER THE POP CULTURE OF EACH GENERATION

Aprons from the Seventies were often gaudy, raunchy, or "cute" to the extreme. Aprons shaped like chaps were worn over pants, and aprons made in the shape of underwear were also not uncommon, and in some cases dabbled in the realm of the naughty, such as one with a zipper labeled "In Case of Fire," which opened to reveal stuffed "private" parts. Other common types of X-rated aprons include commercially printed ones with collages of pornographic, racist, and otherwise offensive cartoons.

left: This Genius at Work apron is made of printed canvas. After World War II, men's aprons became popular, usually sporting barbecue or bartender themes.
right: The gender-neutral shape of this Nineties printed canvas apron is one of the few surviving apron styles today.

above: "Memory aprons" are still given occasionally as gifts, signed by everyone in the recipient's club, work team, or family. On this organdy apron, some names are embroidered; others are simply written with felt marker. This apron is a design typical of the late Forties or early Fifties.

• READ FOR CLUES

If it's a commercially made apron, read the label and find out when that company produced or sold aprons. If you discover a school, laundry, or camp label, find out when the organization was in business. And if you find an original price tag intact, try to determine when aprons sold for that amount.

above: The cut and print of this commercially made polished cotton apron with organdy ruffle places it in the Forties.

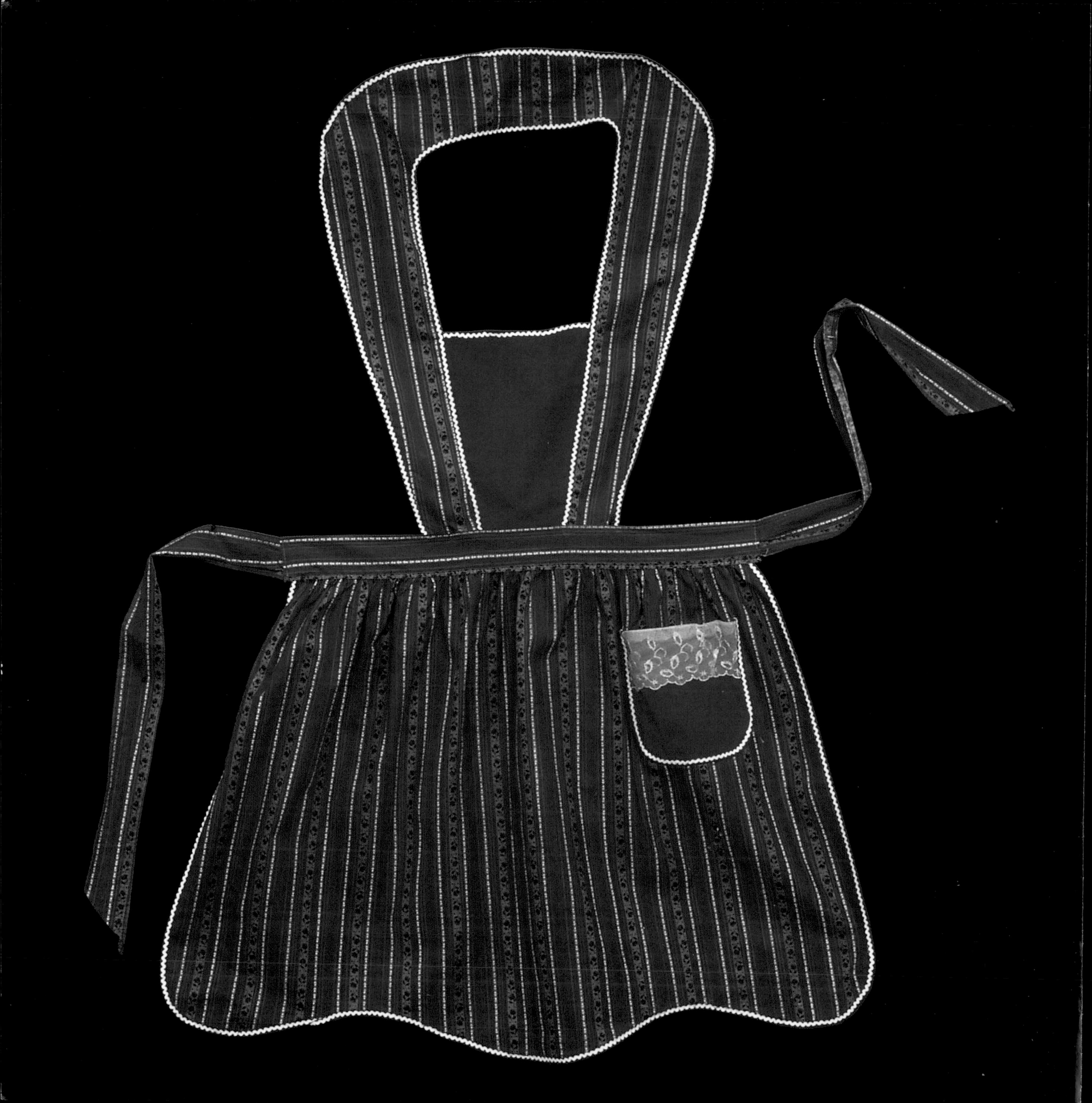

•TALK WITH OTHERS

Ask an elder. When did she wear that style apron? Or ask professionals such as merchants at vintage and antique stores, textile or costume specialists at museums or universities, or costume designers for acting troupes.

opposite: The dark colors, fabric, and design of this apron are all typical of the Forties. The mediocre quality of the eyelit lace pocket trim is also indicative of this decade, as "fine cloth" was hard to come by.
above: The cut and fabric of this apron places it in the Forties when most women's clothing was cut close-fitting to conserve fabric. Apron is shown over a Fifties dress with full skirt and rhinestones.

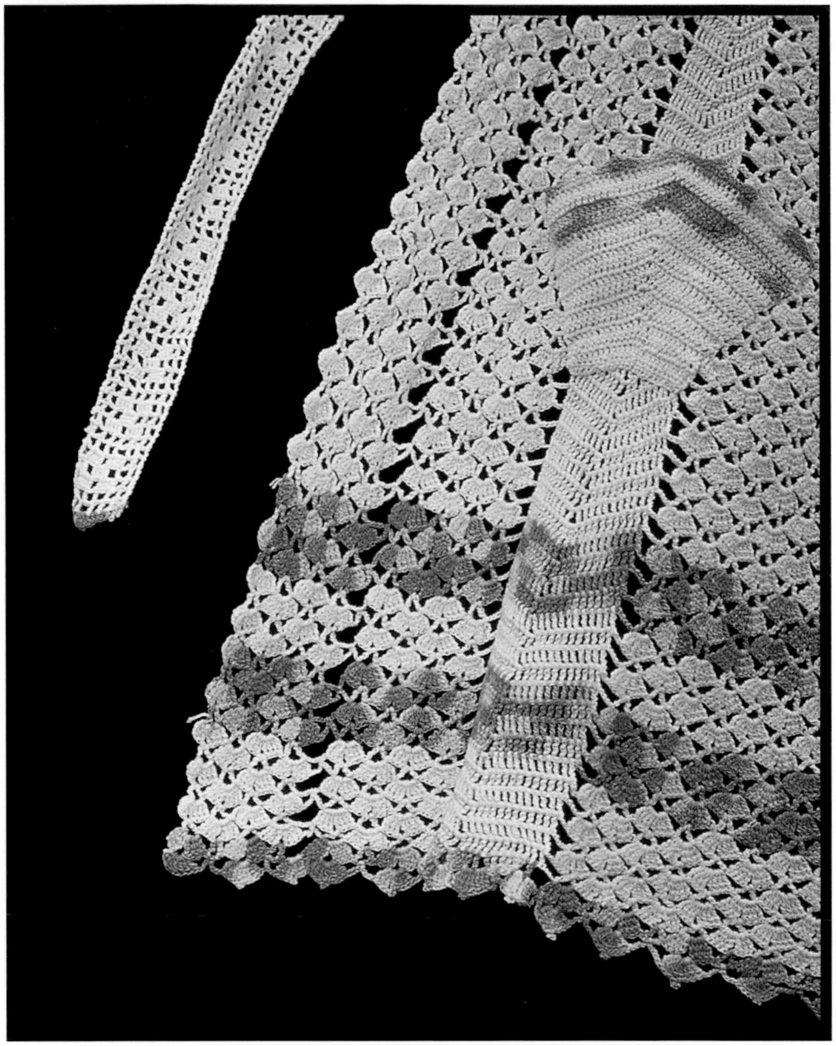

above: Crocheted aprons are hard to date, as crochet was popular from the beginning of the century through the Forties and even into the Sixties. With this apron, length is no clue, as this is a child's apron, but variegated thread became popular in the Forties, so it is most likely from the Forties or Fifties.

• USE YOUR IMAGINATION

If you've gathered all the information you can and the clues don't fall neatly into place, be creative!

below: Three clues indicate this Christmas apron is from the Fifties: it's felt, it's flared to go over a circle skirt, and it has a large sequin decoration, common in that era. Other materials used include beads, bells, and ribbon.

In farm communities, women used their aprons to plant; twenty or more women would line up side by side, each with her pouched apron full of grain, and would sow the freshly plowed fields in unison with the seeds from their aprons.

opposite: After World War II and through the Fifties, fabric was more readily available and colors were brighter. Border prints and anthropomorphized characters were both popular. This flower-themed cotton apron is printed to look like gingham.

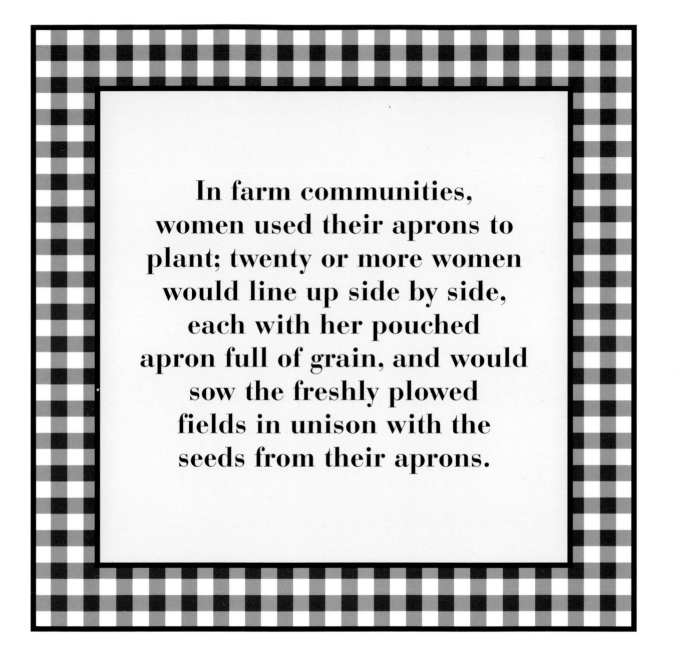

GLOSSARY

Apron
1. an over-garment worn in front to protect clothing or wearer
2. anything like an apron in shape or function
—driveway apron, the end that widens at the street
—stage apron, the part in front of the curtain
—runway apron, the open space in front of the airplane hangar
—machine apron, a machine part that protects other parts
From the French "naperon," a small tablecloth or napkin.

Bib
Part of a full apron covering the wearer's chest

Barbecue apron, bartender's apron, butcher's apron
Full, flat apron with narrow ties originally worn by several trades people, then by men in the Fifties. Today, the most common style for employment or domestic wear by both genders.

Carpenter's apron
Short apron made of thick leather and strapping consisting completely of pockets and tool straps.

Cobbler's apron
A term used to refer to both full aprons and smocks. Sturdy, with pockets across the front just below the waist.

Cocktail apron, tea apron
Decorative half apron.

Four-way apron
Rectangular cloth folded in half with the apron string sewn in at the half-way point. When the wearer ties the apron on, the result is that there are two layers of cloth forming the skirt. The term "four way" comes from the fact that the apron can be worn with four different surfaces being used on the front at different times by reversing the apron and flipping it inside out.

Full apron
Apron that covers the front of a wearer's torso from the upper chest to the knees.

Gore
Triangular piece of material used to give a flair to an apron.

Grandma apron
A full apron made of lightweight cotton, often with small print, such as flowers and edged with bias tape. Apron covers the wearer's front, sides and back and ties in back, with holes for arms and neck. Commonly a work apron, not for entertaining.

Half apron
An apron with waistband and skirt, no bib, practical or decorative.

Hooverette
An apron style introduced during World War I when Herbert Hoover was Food Administrator. Practical, full wraparound apron had two half-fronts that overlapped, tied in back.

Nail apron, change apron
A short, flat apron, skirt consisting wholly of pockets, originally made of canvas and used for holding nails. Now made of various fabrics and used by workers needing pockets, i.e., street vendors, ticket takers, etc.

Pinafore
From "pin afore," as the earliest designs has strapless bibs that were pinned to the front of the primary garment. A type of full apron which was originally worn as a protective garment and which evolved into a decorative accessory. Usually, a full skirt with bib and yoke fully covering the front and back of the wearer's torso but with sides uncovered. Often with ruffles.

Pinnie
Short pinafore covering only the upper body, usually worn by a sports team to distinguish it from the opposing team.

Rickrack
Zigzag braid trimming.

Skirt
The part of an apron below the waist.

Smock
Like a full apron, a smock covers the wearer's front, sides and back and ties in back, with holes for arms and neck. However, a smock is short, extending only approximately eight inches below the waist. Often the lower span is completely filled with pockets.

Split apron
Protective garments worn by some movers, sanitation workers and blacksmiths that are split and tied to each leg. Known as split aprons, they have the same design as chaps.

Yoke
On a full apron with solid upper body coverage rather than neck straps, the yoke is the part that goes over the shoulders.

Related Reading

Carle, Eric. *My Apron: A Story from My Childhood*. New York City: Grosset-Putnam, 1994.
Coontz, Stephanie. *The Way We Never Were: American Families and the Nostalgia Trap*. New York City: Basic Books, 1997.
Cowan, Ruth Schwartz. *More Work for Mother: The Ironies of Household Technology from the Open Hearth to the Microwave*. New York City: Pantheon Books, 1983.
Horsfield, Margaret. *Biting the Dust*. New York City: St. Martin's Press, 1998.
McKissack, Patricia and Fred. *Ma Dear's Aprons*. New York City: Knopf, 1997.
Strasser, Susan. *Never Done: A History of American Housework*. New York City: Pantheon Books, 1982.

ACKNOWLEDGMENTS

Special thanks to:

Barbara Braun, agent extraordinaire, for persevering. They made up the phrase "beyond the call of duty" for her.

Editor Mary McGuire Ruggiero and designer Bryn Ashburn at Running Press, for their skill, patience, and commitment to doing it right all the way down to the details.

Kathryn Adamchick, for seeing the possibilities and adding her magic.

Joile Mackney, proprietor of The Vintage Haberdashery, St. Louis, MO, for so generously providing her aprons, dresses, and expertise.

Rosalie Utterbach, Vilma Matchette, Louise Coffee-Webb and Woodbury University, Burbank, CA, for sharing aprons from the University's collection and for breaking ground with their Ties that Bind apron exhibit in 1990.

Laura Brown, Sharon Graham, Ruth Cobb and Andrea Avery for sharing aprons and stories.

Dr. Annie Valk, for historical consultation.

Sharon Bocklage and Kathe Dunlop for encouragement, editing, and apron sightings.

Bill Russell for cooking dinner and putting up with me when I worked too hard.

Thanks also to:

Lucy Commoner of the Cooper-Hewitt Museum; Rachel Granholm of the American Federation of Arts; Dorothy Globus of the Fashion Institute of Technology; Julia Samerdyke of the Missouri Historical Society; Laura Vookles of the Hudson River Museum; Alan Suits of Coyote's Paw Gallery in St. Louis, Missouri; Becky Homan, Karen Elshout, and Patricia Corrigan of the *St. Louis Post Dispatch*; Jeannette Batz of *The Riverfront Times*; Carolyn Benesh of *Ornament Magazine*; Nancy Lindemeyer and Mary Forsell of *Victoria*; St. Louis Older Women's League; Jean Mallinckrodt, Craig Forwalter, and the Women's Fellowship, Ebenezer United Church of Christ, Augusta, Missouri; Sandy Dijkstra; Beth Alberty; Ginger Carter; Wendy Richards; John Hilgert; Marty and Pam Keeven; Rosanne Weiss; Lynn Wakefield; Nancy and Mimi Margulies; Alan Kaulen; Jennifer Silverberg; John Beatty; Gail Gartelos; Jean Ponzi; Lois Reborn; Geri Redden; Julie Graham; Neysa Chouteau; Libby Reuter; Gianis Lalsandhu; Irene Dickenson; Carrie Dickerson; Marcie Stoyke-Riley; Marie Samuel; Karen Holseth-Broekema; Linda Mueller; Terry Medford; Mayu Desai. The Hearty Girls; the WOWs; and you whose name I have neglected to include but whose contribution I appreciate none the less.

And thanks to all, both credited and anonymous, who shared their aprons and apron memories.

ABOUT THE AUTHOR

Joyce Cheney is a writer, curator, and consultant who lives in the midwest amongst her loved ones and 400 aprons. When working, she wears either a canvas nail apron or a full-length barbecue apron with pockets, and when she wears a dress-up apron, she picks one that goes with her outfit.

Her touring exhibit, "Apron Strings, Ties to the Past," has appeared in more than 15 cities.

PHOTO CREDITS

Mayu Desai, St. Louis, MO: pp 6, 10, 11, 13, 15, 17, 26, 30, 43, 44, 47, 48, 49, 55, 57, 64, 67, 72, 78, 79, 88, 89, 93, 110, 113, 114, 117, 119, 123, 125, 127, 131, 136, 138
Commercial Image, St. Louis, MO: pp 5, 9, 25, 27, 28, 32, 33, 34, 37, 38, 40, 41, 42, 51, 52, 53, 54, 58, 60-61, 63, 66, 69, 70, 73, 74, 75, 77, 80, 83, 84, 85, 86, 90, 94, 96-97, 98, 101, 102, 105, 106, 109, 118, 124, 126, 128, 129, 130, 132, 133, 134, 135, 137, 139, 140, 141

Aprons courtesy of:
Laura Brown: pp 37, 41, 64, 77
Ruth Cobb: pp 34, 69, 73, 84, 124, 141
Coyote's Paw Gallery, St. Louis, MO: pp 88, 89
Etana Finkler: p 136
Sharon Graham: pp 9R, 25UR, 27, 38R, 40, 54, 59, 63, 66, 86L, 134
Gianis Lalsandhu: p 18
Libby Reuter: p 110
Dr. Bill Russell: p 114
The Vintage Haberdashery, St. Louis, MO: pp 106, 133L
Woodbury University, Burbank, CA: pp 6, 10, 11, 13, 15, 26, 28, 30, 38R, 44, 57, 67, 78, 79, 119, 123, 125, 127, 128, 130, 131, 138, 140

All other aprons are from the author's collection.

All dresses courtesy of The Vintage Haberdashery, St. Louis, MO

After my grandmother passed away,
we came upon her dressy aprons.
I saved two of them and wear them at family dinners.
It's a way of keeping Grandma with us.

—W.D. Arminio

My mother always wore an apron
with matching oven mitts when she cooked.
Once she bought an Elvis apron with mitts
that looked like microphones.

—Anonymous

When I was 12, I washed dishes
in an Italian restaurant.
Putting on my apron at the beginning
of my shift transformed me into a focused,
busy child/adult. Then at 15, I waitressed
and got a short, shiny black apron with a
pocket for my pad and pen.

—S. Lang